fact files

CHRIS MATTISON

with Val Davies and
David Alderton

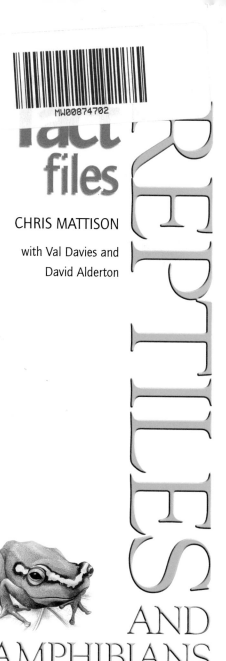

REPTILES
AND
AMPHIBIANS

**CHARTWELL
BOOKS, INC.**

Published by
CHARTWELL BOOKS, INC.
A Division of **BOOK SALES, INC.**
114 Northfield Avenue
Edison, New Jersey 08837

The Brown Reference Group plc
8 Chapel Place
Rivington Street
London EC2A 3DQ
www.brownreference.com

ISBN 0-7858-1968-1

Editorial Director: Lindsey Lowe

Project Director: Graham Bateman

Art Director: Steve McCurdy

Editors: Derek Hall, Virginia Carter

Artists: Denys Ovenden, Philip Hood, Myke Taylor, Ken Oliver,
          Michael Woods, David M. Dennis

Printed in China

Contents

Introduction

For a long part of their history amphibians and reptiles were a much more prominent feature of the Earth's fauna than they are today. For many millions of years reptiles were the dominant forms of life. Both groups, however, have become far less important in terms of numbers of species—today the amphibians (with about 5,350 species) and the reptiles (with 8,000 species) are less numerous than either fish or birds.

Amphibians made the transition from the totally aquatic life of fish to life on land about 365 million years ago in the Devonian Period. Reptiles evolved from amphibians some 340 million years ago, a significant development in their evolution being the laying of amniotic eggs (shelled eggs in which the embryo is surrounded by three special membranes: the amnion, chorion, and allantois). By 310 million years ago these early land-dwelling animals that laid amniotic eggs split into two branches— one that would eventually lead to the mammals and the other to today's reptiles and birds.

There are some similarities between amphibians and reptiles. In their basic forms all have a tail and four legs, although through history tail and limb loss have occurred separately many times. Both groups have a single ventricle in the heart—birds and mammals have two. Also, both are mostly poikilothermic. This means that they are unable to maintain a constant, or near-constant, temperature and therefore have a body temperature similar to that of their surroundings. The term "cold-blooded" is often used to describe this condition, but in reality animals living in tropical climates cannot be said to have "cold blood." Various strategies have evolved, enabling each animal to maintain its preferred body temperature, either warming the body by, for example, basking in the sun or cooling it by seeking shelter.

Amphibians and reptiles differ markedly in two key respects. Amphibians have a soft, smooth skin that is permeable to water and eggs that lack a waterproof layer and must be laid in water or damp places. Reptiles, on the other hand, have coarse, dry scales that are impervious to water, and their eggs have a thick, hard, or parchmentlike shell that holds moisture in, enabling the young to develop inside even on dry land. There are exceptions to these rules. For example, eggs of certain species from both groups may be retained and hatch inside the body of the females, who "give birth" to live young. The significance of these differences is that amphibians are essentially tied to aquatic or damp habitats, while reptiles are also able to live in the hottest and driest places.

About this Book

Just by looking, we can recognize that all snakes are probably related and that crocodiles are quite different from turtles and tortoises. Scientists take this study much further and to minute detail in the science of taxonomy, in which relationships are worked out using a hierarchy of categories known as taxa. Amphibians all belong to the class Amphibia, and reptiles to the class Reptilia. In turn the amphibians are divided into three orders: Gymnophiona (caecilians), Caudata (salamanders and newts), and Anura (frogs and toads). The reptiles are divided into four living orders: Testudines (turtles and tortoises), Squamata (lizards, worm lizards, and snakes), Rhynchocephalia (tuataras), and Crocodylia (crocodiles and alligators). Squamata is traditionally further divided into three suborders: Sauria (lizards), Amphisbaenia (worm lizards), and snakes (Serpentes). Some modern scientists do not use these suborder categories, but they are retained here for convenience.

In this book you will find representatives of all orders and suborders of amphibians and reptiles, which are color coded and listed on pages 3 to 5. Within a suborder such as Serpentes, all vipers and pit vipers are placed in the family Viperidae, and all cobras and allies in the family Elapidae. In all there are some 44 families of amphibians and 56 families of reptiles. Very closely related rattlesnakes, such as the western diamondback and the sidewinder, are all placed in the genus *Crotalus*. Finally, the individual species, such as the western diamondback and the sidewinder, are distinguished by being given the scientific names *Crotalus atrox* and *Crotalus cerastes* respectively.

In *Animal Fact File: Reptiles and Amphibians* you will find illustrated articles on 244 species or groups of reptiles and amphibians arranged by order, suborder, and family. Each article follows a fixed structure. The color-coded header strip denotes the main group to which each animal belongs and gives its common name. The fact panel then lists its scientific name and other taxonomic information. Where the article covers two or more species, the identity of the illustrated animal is given. The next sections describe different features of the animal and its lifestyle.

As with all animals, the survival of many amphibians and reptiles is in doubt as they endure and suffer from the pressures brought on them by humans. Under the heading "Status" information is given about the threats or lack of threat to each animal. (For definitions of the various categories of threat see the IUCN Table in the Glossary on page 253.) Also given is a list of similar species that may be found in the region. Finally, a world map shows the distribution of each species, highlighting its natural range, unless indicated.

Rank	Scientific name	Common name
Kingdom	Animalia	Animals
Phylum	Chordata	Animals with a backbone
Class	Reptilia	Reptiles
Order	Squamata	Lizards, Snakes, Amphisbaenians
Suborder	Serpentes	Snakes
Family	Viperidae	Vipers and Pit Vipers
Genus	*Crotalus*	Rattlesnakes
Species	*Crotalus atrox*	Western diamondback rattlesnake

The kingdom Animalia is subdivided into phyla, classes, orders, families, genera, and species. Above is the classification for the western diamondback rattlesnake.

South American Aquatic Caecilians

Common name South American aquatic caecilians (rubber eels, black eels, Sicilian eels, rubber caecilians)

Scientific name *Typhlonectes* sp.

Family Typhlonectidae (sometimes regarded as a subfamily—Typhlonectinae—of the Caeciliidae)

Order Gymnophiona

Number of species 3

Size 18 in (46 cm) to 22 in (56 cm)

Key features The 3 species are all very similar and almost featureless; long and slender with a smooth, slimy, rubbery skin; eyes very small and barely discernible; no tail; gray or blue-gray in color without markings; similar to an eel but without fins

Habits Completely aquatic and active mostly at night, hiding by day in a burrow or among aquatic vegetation

Breeding Live-bearers with small numbers of young (up to 9); gestation period 215–225 days

Diet Aquatic invertebrates and slow-moving vertebrates; may also scavenge dead animals

Habitat Poorly known but thought to be slow-moving rivers, lakes, and swamps

Distribution Northern South America

Status Probably common

Similar species None, but can be mistaken for eels

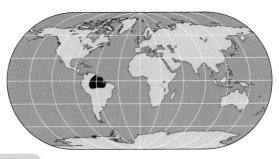

Japanese Giant Salamander

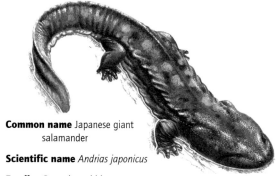

Common name Japanese giant salamander

Scientific name *Andrias japonicus*

Family Cryptobranchidae

Order Caudata (Urodela)

Size 28 in (71 cm) to 39 in (100 cm); exceptionally to 4.6 ft (1.4 m)

Key features Massive salamander with a flattened head and body; eyes tiny with no lids; limbs short and flattened; tail short and oar shaped with high dorsal and ventral fins; rough skin is reddish brown in color with many folds and wrinkles

Habits Aquatic; nocturnal, hiding by day in burrows or rocky crevices

Breeding Female lays 400-600 eggs, which are guarded by a male until they hatch 6 or 7 weeks later

Diet Aquatic vertebrates and invertebrates

Habitat Wide mountain rivers with rocky or gravelly bottoms

Distribution Japan (southwestern Honshu and Kyushu)

Status Vulnerable (IUCN); affected by habitat destruction and pollution of streams

Similar species The Chinese giant salamander, *A. davidianus*, is similar but differs in the pattern of tubercles on its head and throat, and it grows slightly larger than the Japanese species

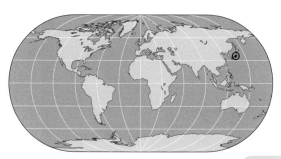

Hellbender

Common name
    Hellbender (mud devil, ground puppy, Allegheny alligator, big water lizard, devil dog)

Scientific name *Cryptobranchus alleganiensis*

Family Cryptobranchidae

Order Caudata (Urodela)

Size 12 in (30 cm) to 29 in (74 cm)

Key features Head and body strongly flattened; there is a wrinkled fold of skin along each flank; eyes small and gray; body yellowish brown or olive-green in color with irregular black spots, some of which may clump together to make larger blotches; eyelids absent

Habits Usually nocturnal; hides by day under rocks and submerged logs but also active in the day during rain, especially in the breeding season

Breeding Fertilization is external; females lay 150–400 eggs in an underground nest

Diet Mainly crayfish; small fish, other hellbenders, tadpoles, toads, and water snakes also recorded

Habitat Clear, fast-flowing mountain streams with no silt

Distribution North America from southern New York State to northern Alabama

Status Formerly common but becoming increasingly rare due to habitat destruction, silting, and pollution of the streams in which it lives

Similar species None in the region; the related giant salamanders of Japan and China (*Andrias japonicus* and *A. davidianus*) are similar but even larger

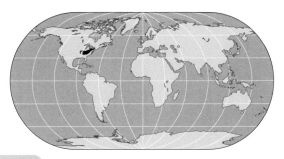

Amphiumas

Two-toed amphiuma
(*Amphiuma means*)

Common name Amphiumas (Congo eels, conger eels, ditch eels)

Scientific name *Amphiuma* sp.

Family Amphiumidae

Order Caudata (Urodela)

Number of species 3 (one-toed amphiuma, *A. pholeter*; two-toed amphiuma, *A. means*; three-toed amphiuma, *A. tridactylum*)

Size Up to 39 in (100 cm)

Key features Very elongated and eel-like; body cylindrical; legs tiny and vestigial with 1, 2, or 3 toes according to species; eyes small with no eyelids; external gills lacking, but pair of gill slits present just behind the head; color gray, paler underneath, with no markings

Habits Completely aquatic

Breeding Females lay long strings of 50–150 eggs and remain with them until they hatch

Diet Almost any aquatic organisms, including crayfish, frogs, fish, water snakes, and snails

Habitat Ponds, ditches, swamps, and slow-moving streams

Distribution Southeastern North America (the coastal plain from eastern Texas to southeastern Virginia)

Status Common (*A. means* and *A. tridactylum*); *A. pholeter* is rare

Similar species The 3 species resemble each other greatly, but otherwise they could only be confused with eels (however, eels have fins, because they are fish)

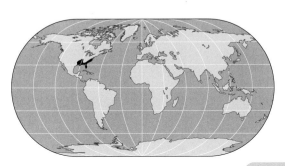

Pacific Giant Salamanders

California giant salamander
(Dicamptodon ensatus)

Common name Pacific giant salamanders

Scientific name *Dicamptodon* sp.

Family Dicamptodontidae

Order Caudata (Urodela)

Number of species 4 (Cope's giant salamender, *D. copei*; coastal giant salamander, *D. tenebrosus*; California giant salamander, *D. ensatus*; Idaho giant salamander, *D. aterrimus*)

Size 7 in (18 cm) to 13 in (33 cm)

Key features Adults large and stout with broad, slightly flattened heads and raised eyes; gray or brown in color, with a dark, mottled pattern; some never metamorphose and remain as large larvae throughout their lives—they have bushy external gills, 4 legs, and low tail fins that start level with the hind limbs

Habits Nocturnal; metamorphosed adults are terrestrial, larvae are aquatic

Breeding Where known, females lay clusters of eggs in underwater cavities

Diet Aquatic and terrestrial invertebrates; larger prey, such as small mammals and lizards; also cannibalistic

Habitat Larvae live in woodland streams; adults live alongside the streams in old-growth forest

Distribution North America in coastal central California and the Pacific Northwest

Status Becoming rarer as their habitat is destroyed by clear-cutting and subsequent silting up of forest streams

Similar species Tiger salamanders, *Ambystoma tigrinum*, are similar but do not occur alongside Pacific salamanders

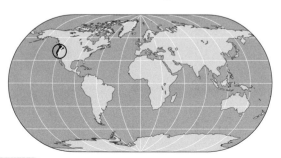

Mudpuppy

Common name
Mudpuppy (waterdog)

Scientific name *Necturus maculosus*

Family Proteidae

Order Caudata (Urodela)

Size 8 in (20 cm) to 20 in (50 cm)

Key features Adults take the form of larvae with 3 pairs of branched, bushy external gills and with tail fins; wide, flat head with small eyes; body flattened from top to bottom; color brown with lighter speckled markings; larvae have a pair of yellow stripes down the back

Habits Totally aquatic; unable to survive long out of water

Breeding External fertilization; female lays her clutches of 60–120 eggs in underwater cavities in the spring or summer; eggs hatch after 38–63 days

Diet Aquatic insects and their larvae, crustaceans, amphibians, and fish

Habitat Rivers, lakes, ditches, and streams

Distribution Eastern North America from southeastern Canada into the eastern United States but not along the coastal plain

Status Common in suitable habitat

Similar species The hellbender, *Cryptobranchus alleganiensis*, lacks external gills as an adult and occupies a different type of habitat; could possibly be confused with other mudpuppies (waterdogs), but they are smaller, their ranges do not overlap, and they are all comparatively rare

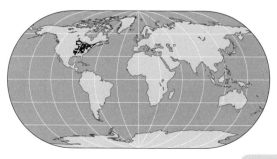

Olm

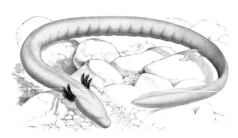

Common name Olm (white salamander, human fish)

Scientific name *Proteus anguinus*

Family Proteidae

Order Caudata (Urodela)

Size 8 in (20 cm) to 12 in (30 cm)

Key features Body elongated with spindly legs and a short tail; head has a blunt, rounded snout; eyes are covered with skin; even adults have bright-red, feathery external gills; body lacks pigment unless it has been exposed to light, in which case it is brown or black; 1 subspecies that lives near the surface is permanently black

Habits Totally aquatic

Breeding Fertilization is internal; females lay up to 70 eggs attached to the underside of a rock

Diet Aquatic invertebrates, especially freshwater shrimp and insect larvae

Habitat Underground streams and lakes in karst limestone formations

Distribution Southern Europe from extreme northeastern Italy through southern Slovenia along the Croatian coast and western Bosnia; also introduced populations in the French Pyrenees

Status Seriously threatened by pollution in many locations

Similar species None

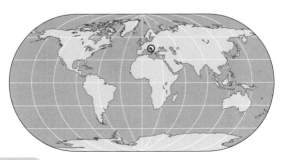

Cascade Torrent Salamander

Common name Cascade torrent salamander

Scientific name *Rhyacotriton cascadae*

Family Rhyacotritonidae

Order Caudata (Urodela)

Size 3 in (7.5 cm) to 4.5 in (11 cm)

Key features Slender salamander with a small head, raised eyes, and a short tail; body yellowish brown above and yellow below with a distinct line where the 2 colors meet; back and sides covered with small dark spots

Habits Secretive and nocturnal, hiding by day under stones at the water's edge

Breeding Fertilization is external; females probably lay their eggs singly; eggs are relatively large

Diet Not known but probably small terrestrial and aquatic invertebrates

Habitat Streams and edges of streams in old-growth forest

Distribution Pacific Northwest (Cascade Mountains in Washington and Oregon)

Status Rare

Similar species 3 other species of *Rhyacotriton* are virtually identical, and identification is only possible through distribution

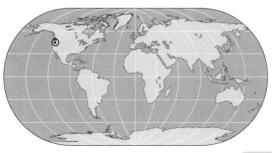

Sirens

Greater siren
(Siren lacertina)

Common name Lesser siren, greater siren

Scientific name *Siren intermedia, Siren lacertina*

Family Sirenidae

Order Caudata (Urodela)

Size Lesser siren: 7 in (18 cm) to 27 in (69 cm); greater siren: 20 in (50 cm) to 35 in (90 cm)

Key features Both species eel-like except for a pair of small front limbs with 4 small toes and feathery external gills; gills are close to the legs and sometimes obscure them; color dark brown or olive with darker spots, sometimes entirely black; larvae and juveniles of the lesser siren often have a red patch on the snout and another along the side of the head

Habits Totally aquatic; nocturnal

Breeding Fertilization probably external; female lesser siren lays 200–550 eggs in a large clump; greater siren lays up to 1,400 eggs singly or in groups; eggs hatch after about 8 weeks

Diet Wide variety of prey taken, including invertebrates, especially insect larvae, snails, crayfish; they also eat some vegetation and amphibian eggs, including their own

Habitat Swamps, marshes, ponds, and ditches—the main requirement being plenty of mud

Distribution Lesser siren: southeastern North America from the Mexican border on the Gulf Coast to southeastern West Virginia and inland along the Mississippi Valley; greater siren: a more limited range within the same area

Status Common in suitable (but dwindling) habitats

Similar species The small front legs and absence of hind legs distinguish them from all salamanders except the dwarf sirens, *Pseudobranchus axanthus* and *P. striatus,* which are much smaller

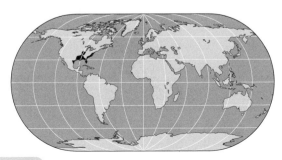

Axolotl

Common name Axolotl (Mexican mole salamander, Mexican walking fish)

Scientific name *Ambystoma mexicanum*

Family Ambystomatidae

Order Caudata (Urodela)

Size 8 in (20 cm) but exceptionally to 12 in (30 cm)

Key features 4 limbs; 3 pairs of feathery external gills; high dorsal and caudal fins; head broad and flat; mouth has a wide gape; eyes small; wild-type axolotls are dark gray in color with scattered, small black spots; laboratory strains may be white or different colors produced by selective breeding

Habits Totally aquatic; more active at night

Breeding Females lay up to 1,000 eggs attached singly or in small clumps to twigs or aquatic plants; eggs hatch after about 2 weeks

Diet Aquatic invertebrates, including insect larvae and worms; fish and tadpoles

Habitat High-altitude lakes

Distribution Lake Xochimilco and Lake Chalco on the central Mexican plateau

Status Protected (CITES); Vulnerable IUCN

Similar species 4 other Mexican *Ambystoma* species (3 from central Mexico and 1 from Puebla) are axolotls and therefore similar in appearance

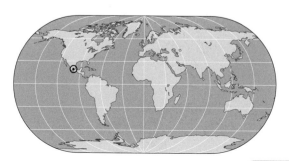

Tiger Salamander

Common name Tiger salamander

Scientific name *Ambystoma tigrinum*

Family Ambystomatidae

Order Caudata (Urodela)

Size 7 in (18 cm) to 14 in (35 cm)

Key features Head broad and flattened; mouth wide, eyes raised; limbs and feet short and stocky; tail relatively short and rounded in cross-section, although it becomes flattened from side to side in breeding males; males have slightly longer tails than females; coloration usually black, gray, or dark brown with lighter markings in yellow or cream or pale brown depending on the subspecies; neotenic individuals are common in some populations

Habits Terrestrial as an adult; nocturnal

Breeding Internal fertilization; females lay clumps of 5–100 eggs (the average is about 50) attached to aquatic plants or twigs; eggs hatch after 20–50 days

Diet Invertebrates and small vertebrates, including other salamanders; cannibalistic individuals occur

Habitat Forests, fields, meadows, and even desert and semidesert areas when breeding pools are available

Distribution North America, almost coast to coast, and from Canada to Central Mexico

Status Generally common, but some forms are extremely rare

Similar species Pacific giant salamanders, *Dicamptodon* species, the spotted salamander, *A. maculatum*, and other well-marked large species could be confused with tiger salamanders

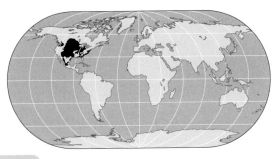

Black-Bellied Salamander

Common name Black-bellied salamander

Scientific name *Desmognathus quadramaculatus*

Subfamily Desmognathinae

Family Plethodontidae

Order Caudata (Urodela)

Size 4 in (10 cm) to 8 in (20 cm)

Key features Stocky; appears rubbery rather than slimy; limbs well developed; 14 conspicuous costal grooves along its flanks; tail is flattened from side to side and has a ridge along the top; mainly brown in color, peppered with small spots of greenish yellow or rust brown, becoming overall darker with age; body black below

Habits Nocturnal; terrestrial or semiaquatic

Breeding Fertilization is internal; female lays small clutches of eggs on the undersides of rocks in shallow water; eggs hatch after 8–12 weeks into free-living, aquatic larvae

Diet Larvae eat small invertebrates, such as mayflies, stoneflies, beetles, ants, and bugs; adults eat a range of terrestrial prey, including other salamanders

Habitat Alongside, at the edge of, or in fast-flowing woodland streams

Distribution North America in the Allegheny Mountains from southern West Virginia to northern Georgia

Status Numerous in suitable habitats

Similar species Plethodontid salamanders can be difficult to tell apart, but the black-bellied salamander is one of the larger, more robust species of *Desmognathus*

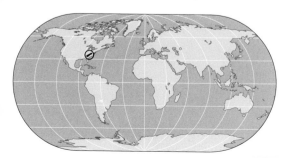

Miniature Salamanders

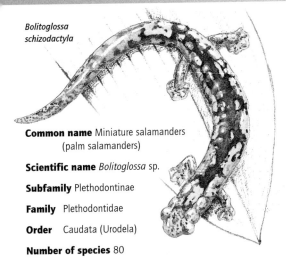

Bolitoglossa schizodactyla

Common name Miniature salamanders (palm salamanders)

Scientific name *Bolitoglossa* sp.

Subfamily Plethodontinae

Family Plethodontidae

Order Caudata (Urodela)

Number of species 80

Size 2.6 in (6.6 cm) to 10.2 in (26 cm) including tail, depending on species

Key features Small- to medium-sized salamanders; body slightly elongated; tail about the same length as their combined head and body; limbs and toes well developed; toes completely or partially webbed; most are some shade of brown, often with lighter brown, buff, or yellow markings along their back

Habits Burrowing, terrestrial, or arboreal species

Breeding Fertilization is internal; eggs undergo direct development and hatch after 4–5 months

Diet Small invertebrates

Habitat Humid forests

Distribution Central and South America

Status Some species are very common, others are known from just a handful of specimens; they are probably not rare, just difficult to find

Similar species Most other plethodontid salamanders from the region are smaller and more slender

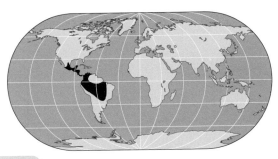

Three-Lined Salamander

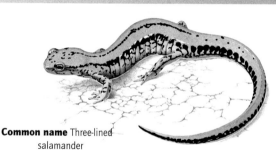

Common name Three-lined salamander

Scientific name *Eurycea guttolineata*

Subfamily Plethodontinae

Family Plethodontidae

Order Caudata (Urodela)

Size 4 in (10 cm) to 7 in (18 cm) including tail

Key features Slender with long tail accounting for 60–65 percent of the total length; limbs well developed; body has a pattern of 3 black stripes, 1 on each flank and 1 down the center of the back, on a tan or light-brown background; central stripe stops at the base of the tail, which is plain brown above

Habits Nocturnal; terrestrial

Breeding Fertilization is internal; female lays up to 100 eggs in winter; eggs hatch after 4–12 weeks

Diet Wide variety of invertebrates, including snails and snail eggs

Habitat Forests; never far from streams, ditches, or ponds

Distribution Southeastern North America along the Appalachian chain onto the Coastal Plain and up the eastern Mississippi Valley as far as southwestern Kentucky

Status Common in suitable habitat

Similar species The species used to be a subspecies of the long-tailed salamander, *E. longicauda*, which is similar and whose range it abuts; the two-lined salamander, *E. bislineata*, is also similar but lacks the dark dorsal stripe

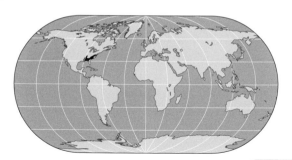

Slimy Salamander

Common name Slimy salamander

Scientific name *Plethodon glutinosus*

Subfamily Plethodontinae

Family Plethodontidae

Order Caudata (Urodela)

Size 4.5 in (11 cm) to 8 in (20 cm)

Key features Body slender; legs well developed; tail is round and about the same length as the head and body combined; color black or dark gray with small silver-white spots over all its surfaces; secretions from its tail give the skin a more slimy appearance than that of other salamanders

Habits Nocturnal; terrestrial

Breeding Fertilization is internal; females suspend clusters of 5–34 eggs from overhanging rocks and coil around them until they hatch after 2–3 months

Diet Invertebrates, especially ants and small beetles, but also a wide variety of other species

Habitat Floors of hardwood forests, swamp forests, and pine woods

Distribution Southeastern North America from Texas and Florida to New York; distribution patchy toward the south of its range

Status Common

Similar species Several other species of *Plethodon*, notably the white-spotted salamander, *P. punctatus*, and the Cumberland Plateau salamander, *P. kentucki*

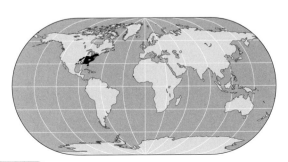

Red Salamander

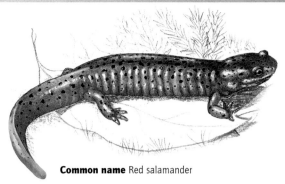

Common name Red salamander

Scientific name *Pseudotriton ruber*

Subamily Plethodontinae

Family Plethodontidae

Order Caudata (Urodela)

Size 3.8 in (9.6 cm) to 7 in (18 cm)

Key features Body stout; tail relatively short compared to many others in the family; skin appears rubbery; color varies from orange to crimson or purplish red; covered with small black spots that are more numerous on the back than the sides; juveniles more brilliantly marked than adults, which become dull with age

Habits Nocturnal; terrestrial or semiaquatic, often living in mud or under logs

Breeding Fertilization is internal; females lay clutches of 70–90 eggs that they attach to the undersides of rocks; they probably brood them until they hatch after about 12 weeks

Diet Small invertebrates and smaller salamanders

Habitat Seepages, streams, and bogs in deciduous forests and meadows

Distribution North America from southern New York to Indiana and the Gulf Coast; absent from much of the Atlantic coastal plain

Status Common in suitable habitat

Similar species The mud salamander, *P. montanus*, is very similar but is usually orange-brown in color

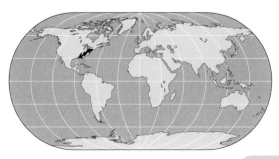

Japanese Fire-Bellied Newt

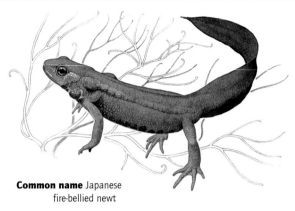

Common name Japanese fire-bellied newt

Scientific name *Cynops pyrrhogaster*

Family Salamandridae

Order Caudata (Urodela)

Size 3.5 in (9 cm) to 4.5 in (11 cm)

Key features Typical newt with a long, flattened tail and 4 well-developed limbs; skin rough; raised parotid gland immediately behind the head; irregular raised ridge along each side of back; color dark chocolate-brown or black, with bright red or orange (occasionally yellow) underside; underside mottled or spotted with the same color as the back

Habits Adults aquatic for most of the year but terrestrial in warm weather

Breeding Fertilization is internal; females attach their eggs to aquatic plants; clutch size may total 324; eggs hatch after about 3 weeks

Diet Invertebrates such as small worms and insects, and their larvae

Habitat Streams and pools in humid regions

Distribution Japan (Honshu, Shikoku, and Kyushu Islands)

Status Common

Similar species Japanese sword-tailed newt, *C. ensicauda*, is larger and has white markings on its flanks; 5 other species of fire-bellied newts also live in China

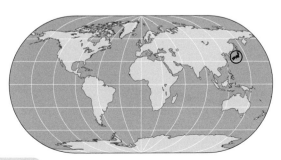

Pyrenean Brook Salamander

Common name Pyrenean brook salamander

Scientific name *Euproctus asper*

Family Salamandridae

Order Caudata (Urodela)

Size 6 in (15 cm)

Key features Body stout; head flat; eyes small; neck has no glands; skin is covered with many small, horny-tipped warts; tail flattened and accounts for about half the total length, slightly longer in males than in females; color olive-brown, gray, or brown, often with dirty yellow spots and stripes; yellow stripe sometimes runs along the dorsal midline, especially in juveniles

Habits Mainly aquatic; nocturnal

Breeding Fertilization is internal; female lays 20–40 eggs and places them in crevices or attaches them to stones; eggs hatch after about 6 weeks

Diet Aquatic invertebrates

Habitat Mountain streams and cool lakes at high altitudes

Distribution Pyrenees Mountains on the border of Spain and France

Status Common in suitable habitat

Similar species The sharp-ribbed newt, *Pleurodeles waltl*, is similar in color but does not live in the Pyrenees; 2 other brook salamanders, *E. montanus* and *E. platycephalus*, live on Corsica and Sardinia respectively

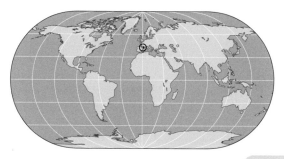

Eastern Newt

Red eft stage

Common name Eastern newt (red-spotted newt)

Scientific name *Notophthalmus viridescens*

Family Salamandridae

Order Caudata (Urodela)

Size 2.5 in (6.3 cm) to 4.5 in (11 cm)

Key features Small newt with velvety skin; tail accounts for about half the total length and has a narrow keel above and below; adults are olive above and yellow below with both surfaces speckled with tiny black flecks; row of small, round, bright-red spots bordered with black on each side, sometimes joined together to form broken stripes; juveniles bright to dull orange (red eft stage)

Habits Aquatic, semiaquatic, and terrestrial depending on stage of life and other factors

Breeding Fertilization is internal; females lay eggs singly over a long period; total eggs laid can number 25–350; eggs hatch after 20–35 days

Diet Small invertebrates on the land and in water

Habitat Permanent and semipermanent ponds, lakes, reservoirs, ditches, and swamps in forests or open farmland

Distribution Eastern North America

Status Very common

Similar species 2 other species of *Notophthalmus* are similar but lack the small red markings

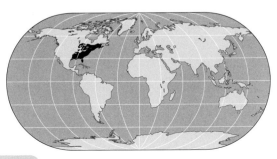

Sharp-Ribbed Newt

Common name Sharp-ribbed newt (Spanish sharp-ribbed newt)

Scientific name *Pleurodeles waltl*

Family Salamandridae

Order Caudata (Urodela)

Size 6 in (15 cm) to 12 in (30 cm)

Key features Stocky newt; face resembles a toad (flattened, rounded, warty, with small eyes on top); entire body is covered with small granules, each with a black horny tip; a row of larger orange poison glands runs down each flank, marking the ends of its ribs; tail accounts for about half its total length and is flattened from side to side

Habits Highly aquatic but sometimes migrates across land if its habitat dries up

Breeding Fertilization is internal; females lay large numbers of eggs, scattering them over a wide area; eggs hatch after 5–14 days

Diet Invertebrates, including tadpoles, and small vertebrates

Habitat Almost any lowland body of water, including ponds, ditches, wells, sluggish rivers, and streams, especially if choked with vegetation

Distribution Spain and Portugal, except the north, and the coastal plain of northern Morocco

Status Very common

Similar species The related *P. poireti* lives in northern Algeria and northern Tunisia

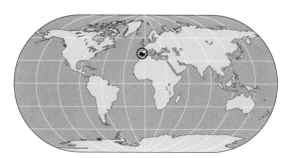

Fire Salamander

Common name Fire salamander

Scientific name *Salamandra salamandra*

Family Salamandridae

Order Caudata (Urodela)

Size 7 in (18 cm) to 11 in (28 cm)

Key features Body chunky; tail short and round in cross-section; limbs stocky; toes stumpy; head wide; skin rubbery both in appearance and in feel; most forms are glossy jet black with markings of various shapes, usually bright yellow but occasionally red or orange; in some forms the yellow markings almost or completely cover the body

Habits Secretive and nocturnal but sometimes active in the day during rainy or misty weather

Breeding Variable; mating takes place on the land; the female usually gives birth to aquatic larvae, but some forms give birth to live juveniles; gestation period very variable

Diet Insects and worms

Habitat Forests of all kinds, usually in hilly or mountainous regions; lightly wooded valleys with streams; rarely found in and around montane lakes

Distribution Europe, with closely related species in North Africa and western Asia

Status Locally common

Similar species Other members of the genus can resemble certain forms, but there is no overlap between species

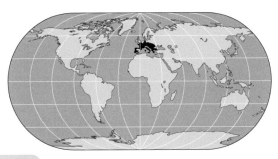

Rough-Skinned Newt

Common name Rough-skinned newt

Scientific name *Taricha granulosa*

Family Salamandridae

Order Caudata (Urodela)

Size 6.1 in (15.5 cm) to 8.6 in (22 cm)

Key features Heavily built newt; skin rough due to its covering of small warts; color dark brown or black with an orange or yellow underside, sometimes with a few dark markings

Habits Adults and juveniles terrestrial; larvae aquatic; adults secretive, emerging at night to feed

Breeding Fertilization is internal and follows courtship in which amplexus takes place; female lays eggs that she attaches singly to aquatic plants or debris

Diet Small invertebrates, such as insects and worms; frogs' eggs and tadpoles

Habitat Damp forests, sometimes fields and meadows, in hilly or mountainous countryside; larvae live in temporary or permanent ponds, lakes, and ditches

Distribution Western North America from southeastern Alaska to San Francisco Bay but not extending far inland

Status Common

Similar species 2 related species, the red-bellied newt, *T. rivularis*, and the California newt, *T. torosa*, live in the same region; they are all very similar, but *T. rivularis* has a rich red underside (the others have orange bellies), and *T. torosa* has larger eyes; distinguishing the latter species from *T. granulosa* in places where they both occur is difficult

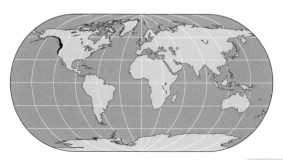

Smooth Newt

Common name Smooth newt
(common newt)

Scientific name *Triturus vulgaris*

Family Salamandridae

Order Caudata (Urodela)

Size 4.5 in (11 cm)

Key features Small newt; skin smooth and slightly velvety when
seen on land; color yellowish brown with small black
flecks on the back; in the breeding season males develop
larger black blotches and a high, wavy crest; underside
in both sexes yellow or orange along the center, fading
to pale yellow or white at the edges

Habits Secretive and nocturnal while on land; in water they can
often be seen surfacing and displaying to each other
during the day

Breeding Fertilization is internal and takes place in the spring;
females lay 200-300 single eggs that hatch after 10-20
days

Diet Small invertebrates

Habitat On land they live in damp places, including woods,
fields, gardens, and parks; in their aquatic (breeding)
phase they use a wide variety of water bodies, including
cattle troughs, garden ponds, and the edges of
larger lakes

Distribution Central and northern Europe from the British Isles
to the Balkans, extending into western Asia north of the
Ural Mountains

Status Common

Similar species The palmate newt, *T. helveticus*, is very similar
out of the breeding season, and females are almost
indistinguishable; several other small newts occur within
the same region

Tailed Frog

Common name Tailed frog

Scientific name *Ascaphus truei*

Family Ascaphidae (sometimes placed in the Leiopelmatidae)

Order Anura

Size From 1 in (2.5 cm) to 2 in (5 cm)

Key features Fairly ordinary looking; skin slightly rough; body brown, olive, gray, or reddish-brown with some irregular mottling; dark stripe through the eye; males have a short "tail" consisting of an extension of the cloaca used for transferring sperm into the cloaca of females; eardrum lacking

Habits Nocturnal; semiaquatic or terrestrial

Breeding Very unusual; fertilization is internal; females lays 40–80 eggs that hatch after about 30 days; larvae take several years to metamorphose

Diet Invertebrates

Habitat Cold, clear, rocky streams flowing through ancient forests

Distribution North America (Pacific Northwest from southern British Columbia, Canada, to northern California), with many separated populations

Status Rare and endangered in Canada (and protected nationally) but no protection in the U.S.

Similar species A second species, *A. montanus*, the Rocky Mountain tailed frog, is sometimes recognized, but it differs only slightly from *A. truei*

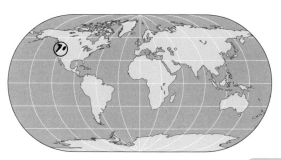

New Zealand Frogs

Common name
New Zealand
frogs

Scientific name
Leiopelma sp.

Family Leiopelmatidae

Hochstetter's frog
(Leiopelma hochstetteri)

Order Anura

Number of species 4 (Hamilton's frog, *L. hamiltoni*; Hochstetter's frog, *L. hochstetteri*; Maud Island frog, *L. pakeka*; Archey's frog, *L. archeyi*)

Size From 1.2 in (3 cm) to 1.9 in (4.8 cm)

Key features Small frogs; mostly brown, sometimes with a reddish or greenish hue; tympanum (external eardrum) and vocal sac absent; toes only slightly webbed; eyes large with vertically elliptical pupils

Habits Very secretive and rarely seen; live under rocks and logs; active only at night

Breeding Females lay clusters of 2–11 eggs in damp places; 5–6 weeks later eggs develop directly into froglets

Diet Small invertebrates

Habitat Rock piles and leaf litter

Distribution New Zealand (2 species in the north of North Island, 1 or 2 species on islands in the Cook Straits)

Status 1 or 2 species listed as Endangered (IUCN); Hamilton's frog, *L. hamiltoni*, is one of the world's rarest species, the others are fairly widespread

Similar species None, but closely related to the tailed frog, *Ascaphus truei*, of North America

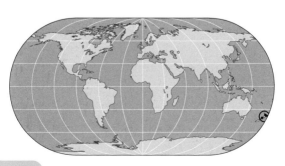

Parsley Frog

Common name
Parsley frog

Scientific name
Pelodytes punctatus

Family Pelodytidae

Order Anura

Size 2 in (5 cm) maximum

Key features Body slender; toes and limbs long; little or no webbing to toes; eyes large with vertical pupils; warts scattered over its back, sometimes arranged in irregular lines; color pale brown, buff, or gray with randomly distributed bright-green or olive spots

Habits Nocturnal; terrestrial; swims and climbs well

Breeding Takes place throughout spring and summer in small, often temporary ponds and ditches; female lays 40–360 eggs in a string; eggs hatch after 3–19 days

Diet Small invertebrates

Habitat Open woods, cultivated land, at the base of walls and rock piles, especially in sandy regions

Distribution Europe (France, northern and eastern Spain, and extreme northwestern Italy)

Status Has become scarce

Similar species The Iberian parsley frog, *P. ibericus* from southern Spain and Portugal, a recently separated species (2000), is similar but smaller and with a different call; also the Caucasian parsley frog, *P. caucasicus*

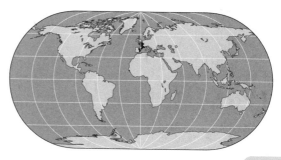

Mexican Burrowing Frog

Common name Mexican
burrowing frog

Scientific name *Rhinophrynus dorsalis*

Family Rhinophrynidae

Order Anura

Size From 2.5 in (6.5 cm) to 3 in (7.5 cm)

Key features Adult body almost as broad as it is long; head tiny
and blunt; snout cone shaped; limbs short, better suited
to burrowing than locomotion; dark gray in color with a
few scattered white or pinkish-white spots around its
face and on its flanks; conspicuous orange or pink stripe
down the center of its back

Habits Strictly burrowing; emerges only during heavy rain

Breeding In temporary pools and flooded fields after heavy rain;
female lays thousands of small eggs that hatch after a
few days

Diet Ants, termites, and their larvae

Habitat Lowland forests and coastal plains

Distribution Central America, barely entering the United States
along the Gulf Coast of Texas, extending along the east
coast of Mexico into the Yucatán Peninsula, Costa Rica,
and just into northeastern Honduras

Status Common but rarely seen

Similar species None; some of the narrow-mouthed toads
(family Microhylidae) have the same body shape, but
they are significantly smaller and lack the brightly
colored dorsal stripe

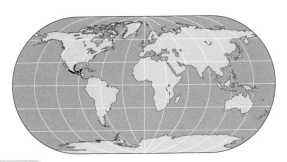

Oriental Fire-Bellied Toad

Common name Oriental fire-bellied toad

Scientific name *Bombina orientalis*

Family Bombinatoridae

Order Anura

Size 2 in (5 cm)

Key features A warty-backed toad with a slightly flattened head and prominent eyes; its back is bright green with irregular black spots, some of which are elongated; underside is bright scarlet with a varying number of black spots and markings; the tips of its toes are also bright red; males have more heavily built forearms than females and develop spiny patches on their hands during the breeding season

Habits Aquatic, usually resting at the water's surface; sometimes active on land

Breeding Clutches of 50–100 eggs are laid singly and sink to the bottom of shallow pools; females may breed repeatedly throughout the spring and summer

Diet Invertebrates, especially flying insects and aquatic insect larvae

Habitat Open shallow ponds, ditches, streams, and flooded fields, including paddy fields

Distribution Eastern China, Korea

Status Thought to be common

Similar species None in the region; The giant fire-bellied toad, *B. maxima*, also from China, has a gray back, and its warts are numerous and larger

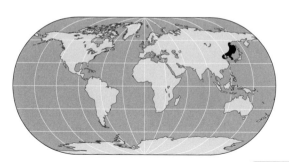

Midwife Toad

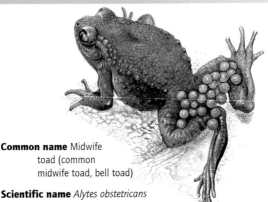

Common name Midwife toad (common midwife toad, bell toad)

Scientific name *Alytes obstetricans*

Family Discoglossidae

Order Anura

Size From 1.5 in (3.8 cm) to 2 in (5 cm)

Key features Body plump and rounded; limbs short; eyes prominent with vertical pupils; a row of small wartlike glands runs down each side of its back, and there is a larger gland behind each eye; body color pale gray, brown, or olive with randomly scattered small, dark markings; warts may be pinkish or yellow in color

Habits Nocturnal and terrestrial; usually hides under stones, logs, or in crevices by day; may dig a short burrow with its front limbs

Breeding Takes place in springtime and on land; male carries the eggs until they hatch after 3–8 weeks

Diet Small invertebrates

Habitat Varied, including open woods, fields, parks, old quarries, and drystone walls

Distribution Europe from the northern half of Spain and Portugal through France and Belgium and into southern Netherlands and parts of Germany and Switzerland; several well-established, introduced colonies in England

Status Common in suitable habitats but disappearing rapidly in the north of their range through habit disturbance and possibly climate change

Similar species There are 3 other midwife toads in the genus; 1 is confined to the island of Majorca, but the others could be mistaken for this one where their ranges overlap

Asian Horned Toad

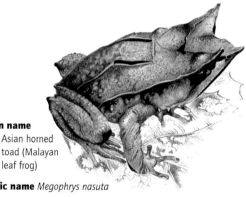

Common name
Asian horned
toad (Malayan
leaf frog)

Scientific name *Megophrys nasuta*

Family Megophryidae

Order Anura

Size From 2.5 in (7.5 cm) to 5 in (13 cm)

Key features Head wide with pointed extensions over eyes and
snout; eyes huge and black; black "mask" on either side
of its head; body shape and coloration cryptic,
resembling a dead leaf with ridges that look like leaf
veins running up the back and irregular black patches
on the back, imitating holes in a leaf

Habits Nocturnal; terrestrial

Breeding In relatively still pools and backwaters along forest
streams

Diet Large invertebrates and small vertebrates, including
smaller frogs

Habitat Tropical rain forests

Distribution Sumatra, Borneo, and the Malaysian Peninsula

Status Common in suitable habitat but rarely seen

Similar species Other species of *Megophrys* are smaller with
smaller skin projections over their eyes; the Solomon
Islands leaf frog, *Ceratobatrachus guentheri*, is similar in
shape, but its range does not overlap that of *Megophrys*

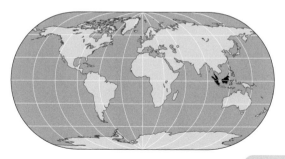

Common Spadefoot

Common name Common spadefoot toad

Scientific name *Pelobates fuscus*

Family Pelobatidae

Order Anura

Size 3 in (7.5 cm)

Key features Body plump and smooth skinned; eyes large and prominent with copper-colored irises and vertical pupils; head has a bony lump on top; back feet are fully webbed and have a "spade" in the form of a crescent-shaped, sharp-edged tubercle on the "heel"; overall dark to light brown in color but sometimes gray or yellowish with darker markings; spade is light in color

Habits Burrowing; mostly nocturnal but sometimes diurnal in the breeding season

Breeding Amplexus is inguinal; females lay 1,000–3,500 eggs that hatch after 4–10 days

Diet Insects and other small invertebrates

Habitat Lowlands on dunes, heaths, pine forests, and fields

Distribution Central and eastern Europe from France to the Ural Mountains; also in the Po Valley in northern Italy

Status Common

Similar species The western spadefoot, *P. cultripes*, occurs in Spain, Portugal, and extreme southwestern France; the eastern spadefoot, *P. syriacus*, lives in Greece, Turkey, and neighboring parts of southeastern Europe; however, their ranges do not overlap with the common spadefoot

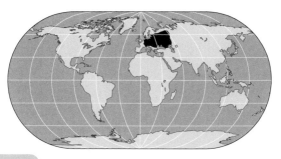

Couch's Spadefoot

Common name
Couch's
spadefoot

Scientific name
Scaphiopus couchi

Family Pelobatidae

Order Anura

Size From 2.3 in (5.5 cm) to 3.5 in (9 cm)

Key features Body plump with soft, fairly smooth skin; eyes
large with yellow irises and vertically elliptical pupils;
limbs short and powerful; hind limbs have hard black
ridges on their "heels," used for burrowing backward into
the ground; color yellowish or greenish brown; females
have brown mottled markings on the back but males are
plain; underside of males and females mostly white;
females larger than males

Habits Nocturnal; terrestrial, spending most of their life
underground

Breeding In temporary pools following rain; females lay up to
3,000 eggs that hatch within a few days

Diet Invertebrates

Habitat Plains, vegetated deserts, and other semiarid places

Distribution Southern United States and northern Mexico,
including Baja California

Status Common but rarely seen

Similar species There are a number of other spadefoot toads in
North America, but Couch's is the only yellow one

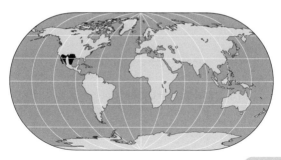

Surinam Toad

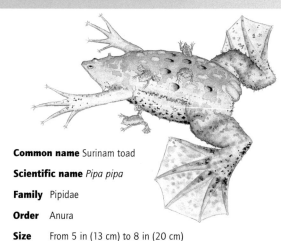

Common name Surinam toad

Scientific name *Pipa pipa*

Family Pipidae

Order Anura

Size From 5 in (13 cm) to 8 in (20 cm)

Key features Body flat and rectangular when seen from above; head triangular with tiny eyes; hind legs thickly built, ending in massive webbed feet; front limbs are thinner and end in elongated fingers with no webbing; back and sides are sprinkled with tubercles and flaps that help disguise the outline; color brown or grayish brown with irregular mottled markings, making it look like a dead leaf

Habits Completely aquatic

Breeding Female lays 80–100 eggs and carries them on her back until they hatch into miniature toads after about 11–19 weeks

Diet Aquatic invertebrates, fish, and tadpoles

Habitat Black-water streams and oxbow lakes with tea-colored water due to decayed organic material

Distribution Northern South America as far south as Amazonian Ecuador; also Trinidad in the West Indies

Status Probably common

Similar species 6 other species in the genus, but they are mostly smaller

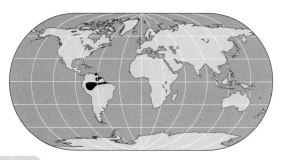

African Clawed Toad

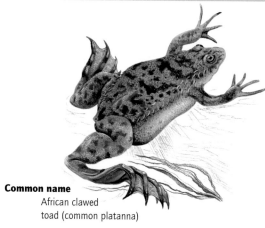

Common name
African clawed
toad (common platanna)

Scientific name *Xenopus laevis*

Family Pipidae

Order Anura

Size From 2.5 in (6 cm) to 5 in (13 cm)

Key features Body roughly pear shaped when seen from above
but slightly flattened from top to bottom; hind legs are
powerful with massive webbed feet, the 3 innermost
toes of which end in small black, horny claws; front legs
are smaller, and fingers are not webbed; eyes are small,
upward pointing, and have rounded pupils and no
eyelids; color brown or gray; limited ability for body to
become lighter or darker according to conditions

Habits Completely aquatic; may move from one pond to
another by "swimming" across the ground during
heavy rain

Breeding Amplexus is inguinal; eggs laid on aquatic vegetation

Diet Anything that will fit into its mouth

Habitat Any body of water no matter how large, small, or
stagnant

Distribution Most of Africa south of the Sahara

Status Extremely common

Similar species Other species of *Xenopus* are similar, although
some have distinctive markings; *Silurana* species are also
similar but have a 4th horny claw

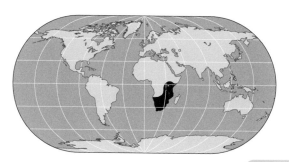

European Common Toad

Common name European common toad

Scientific name *Bufo bufo*

Family Bufonidae

Order Anura

Size From 3 in (8 cm) to 8 in (20 cm)

Key features Typical toad body with warty skin and short back legs; drab brown, gray, or reddish in color with no markings; eyes beautiful and copper colored; parotid glands are large, elongated, and slightly crescent shaped; females are significantly larger than males; males have thicker forearms but no vocal sac

Habits Terrestrial; mainly nocturnal but sometimes active on damp, overcast days or when moving to breeding sites

Breeding An explosive breeder in spring; female lays 3,000–8,000 eggs that hatch after 2–3 weeks

Diet Invertebrates, including insects, earthworms, and slugs

Habitat Very adaptable; common in gardens and other disturbed habitats; also in sparse woodland, meadows, and heaths

Distribution Throughout most of Europe except the extreme north of Scandinavia, Ireland, and some Mediterranean islands; also found in northwest Africa and throughout Central Asia to eastern Siberia

Status Common

Similar species The natterjack toad, *B. calamita*, is smaller, with a yellow stripe down the center of its back and pinkish warts on its flanks; the green toad, *B. viridis*, has green or olive blotches on a putty-colored background

Cane Toad

Common name Cane toad (marine toad, giant toad)

Scientific name *Bufo marinus*

Family Bufonidae

Order Anura

Size 4 in (10 cm) to 9.5 in (24 cm); the largest wild specimen weighed 3 lb (1.36 kg)

Key features Very large, possibly the world's largest toad; head large; neck bears elongated parotid glands; hind thighs have large poison glands; the whole of the back liberally sprinkled with warts; color brown, often plain, but sometimes with a pattern of slightly darker blotches

Habits Nocturnal; terrestrial

Breeding In water; females lay up to 35,000 eggs in a long string; eggs hatch within 48 hours; tadpoles metamorphose in 12–60 days

Diet Most edible things, including insects, small vertebrates, and even dog food

Habitat Absent from very few habitats within its range, including villages and towns

Distribution Natural distribution is Central and South America, just reaching the United States in extreme southern Texas; it has been deliberately introduced to numerous other countries, notably Australia

Status Common, to plague proportions in places

Similar species Several other large brown toads that live in the same region, including the rococo toad, *B. paracnemis*

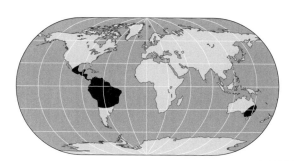

Green Toad

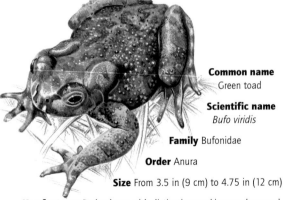

Common name Green toad

Scientific name *Bufo viridis*

Family Bufonidae

Order Anura

Size From 3.5 in (9 cm) to 4.75 in (12 cm)

Key features Body plump with distinctive markings and covered with warts of varying sizes, some of which are pinkish; buff or light gray in color, scattered with large, irregular olive or green blotches; some individuals have a narrow yellow line running down the middle of the back; parotid glands long and narrow; pupils horizontal; females larger than males

Habits Nocturnal and terrestrial; hides in burrows at night or if the weather is too hot or too cold

Breeding Takes place in spring in ponds, ditches, and flooded areas; female lays 2,000–3,000 eggs that hatch after 3–6 days; tadpoles metamorphose after 2–3 months

Diet Invertebrates, including worms and insects; high proportion of adult diet is ants

Habitat Often lives in dry places, especially where the soil is sandy, including open woodland, dunes, cultivated fields, such as rice fields, and around villages

Distribution Eastern Europe from Denmark and southern Sweden across to the Balkans and Russia into western and Central Asia; also the Balearic Islands, Corsica, Sardinia, and North Africa

Status Common

Similar species The natterjack toad, *B. calamita*, is its closest relative but usually has a distinct yellow stripe down its back and lacks the prominent greenish blotches; spadefoot toads (family Pelobatidae) are superficially similar but have vertical pupils

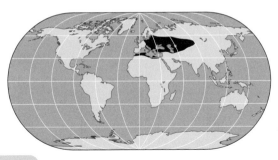

Bell's Horned Frog

Common name Bell's horned frog (Argentine horned frog, escuerzo)

Scientific name *Ceratophrys ornata*

Family Leptodactylidae

Order Anura

Size 5 in (13 cm)

Key features Very distinctive; body plump, almost spherical and nearly as wide as it is long; legs short; mouth huge, stretching the full width of the body; eyes situated toward the top of the head, with small fleshy projections, or horns, over them; color brown, green, or reddish, with darker brown markings consisting of blotches and streaks, sometimes with pale borders

Habits Terrestrial; never very active but more likely to be seen on the move at night

Breeding Seasonal; female lays 1,000–2,000 eggs in ponds and flooded areas during the wet season

Diet Any living thing that fits into its mouth

Habitat Open forests and semidesert flatlands

Distribution Argentina, Paraguay, Uruguay, and southern Brazil

Status Common

Similar species There are 7 other species in the genus, all of similar build, but the coloration and distribution of Bell's horned frog set it apart from the others

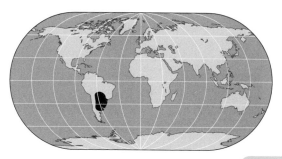

Dwarf Budgett's Frog

Common name Dwarf Budgett's frog

Scientific name *Lepidobatrachus llanensis*

Family Leptodactylidae

Order Anura

Size From 2.5 in (6 cm) to 4 in (10 cm)

Key features Body large, stout, and slightly flattened; limbs short; head broader than its length; eyes and nostrils positioned on top of head, pointing upward; pupils are vertically elliptical; back is covered in irregular small warts and is uniform in color, usually gray but sometimes reddish-brown

Habits Aquatic

Breeding In shallow pools; female can lay over 1,000 eggs that hatch into tadpoles

Diet Large invertebrates and small vertebrates, including smaller frogs

Habitat Temporary shallow pools in seasonally wet floodplains, known as the Chaco region

Distribution Argentina and northern Paraguay

Status Common at times but vulnerable to habitat changes

Similar species Two other species in the genus, *L. laevis* and *L. asper*, are similar in general appearance but differ in their proportions and their pupil shapes; *L. laevis* is also significantly larger

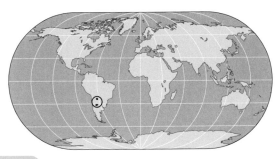

South American Bullfrog

Common name South American bullfrog (smoky mountain frog, mountain chicken, and others)

Scientific name *Leptodactylus pentadactylus*

Family Leptodactylidae

Order Anura

Size From 3.5 in (9 cm) to 8 in (20 cm)

Key features A large and powerful frog; back legs long and muscular; eyes large and positioned on top of head; pupils horizontally elliptical; eardrum is about the same size as the eyes and very prominent; body color varies, but there is usually an orange area on the flanks and groin; otherwise it may be brown, tan, or yellowish with darker markings

Habits Rarely found far from water; nocturnal

Breeding In ponds and lakes during the rainy season; female lays about 1,000 eggs; tadpoles metamorphose after about 4 weeks

Diet Invertebrates and small vertebrates, including other frogs

Habitat Large and small ponds; swamps and neighboring forests, plantations, and clearings in lowland forests

Distribution Central and South America from Honduras to Peru and Brazil

Status Common

Similar species Several other *Leptodactylus* species are similar in appearance, but none grows as large

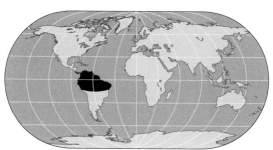

Australian Toadlets

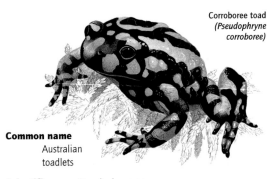

Corroboree toad
(*Pseudophryne
corroboree*)

Common name
Australian
toadlets

Scientific name *Pseudophryne* sp.

Family Myobatrachidae

Order Anura

Number of species 13

Size From 1.2 in (3 cm) to 1.6 in (4 cm)

Key features Body stout; limbs short; skin slightly warty; parotid
glands small; all family members have bold black-and-
white marbling on the underside; some are also brightly
marked above; webbing between digits lacking

Habits Nocturnal; diurnal; some species burrow, but most
are terrestrial

Breeding Female lays 6–40 eggs in damp soil or moss; eggs
hatch after 4–6 months

Diet Small insects, including ants and termites

Habitat Varied; often under rocks and logs in dry or moist
woodland, in flooded grasslands and marshes, and in
sphagnum bogs; sometimes occur at high altitudes

Distribution Found in every state in Australia, including
Tasmania, but more common in the humid southeast
and southwest

Status Some species are endangered; the corroboree toad,
P. corroboree, is thought to be one of Australia's most
endangered frogs

Similar species Several other genera of similar small frogs live
in Australia, and *Pseudophryne* can only be separated
by a combination of characteristics including body
shape, lack of webbing between the toes, small or
absent parotid glands, and bright coloration

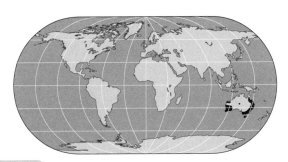

Gastric-Brooding Frog

Common name
Gastric-brooding frog

Scientific name *Rheobatrachus silus*

Family Myobatrachidae

Order Anura

Size From 1.6 in (4 cm) to 2 in (5 cm)

Key features Rather nondescript; snout short; eyes large and dark; body moderately plump; legs of average size; hind feet fully webbed; back is slightly granular and brown or dark brown in color with indistinct dark blotches

Habits Nocturnal; aquatic; shelter under rocks during the day and sit partially submerged on them at night

Breeding Female swallows eggs; development takes place in her stomach; she "gives birth" to between 21 and 26 live froglets via her mouth

Diet Probably small invertebrates

Habitat Fast-flowing, rocky mountain streams running through wet forests

Distribution Australia (the Conondale Mountains, Queensland)

Status Probably extinct

Similar species The other gastric-brooding frog, *R. vitellinus*, was found farther north and was larger; it too is probably extinct

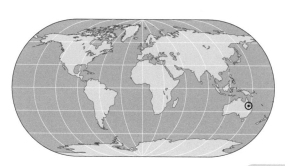

Tomato Frog

Common name Tomato frog

Scientific name *Dyscophus antongilii*

Subfamily Dyscophinae

Family Microhylidae

Order Anura

Size Males to 2.5 in (6 cm); females to just over 4 in (10 cm)

Key features A large red frog; body wide; head narrow; snout bluntly tapering; eyes large and prominent, giving a permanently "surprised" expression; skin smooth except for a pair of fleshy ridges (the dorsolateral folds) running along either side of the back; sometimes small black markings present on its flanks and hind limbs

Habits Terrestrial; nocturnal

Breeding In permanent and temporary pools; female lays over 1,000 eggs; metamorphosis takes about 45 days

Diet Invertebrates

Habitat Forest clearing and sparsely wooded scrub

Distribution Madagascar; only in the northeast, around the Bay of Antongil

Status Rare; because of its limited range and its appeal to collectors, it is internationally protected; Vulnerable (IUCN), CITES (Appendix I)

Similar species There are 2 other species of *Dyscophus*, but they are not likely to be confused with the tomato frog; juveniles can be confused with the burrowing frogs, *Scaphiophryne* sp.

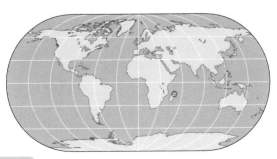

Great Plains Narrow-Mouthed Toad

Common name
Great Plains narrow-mouthed toad
(western narrow-mouthed toad)

Scientific name *Gastrophryne olivacea*

Subfamily Microhylinae

Family Microhylidae

Order Anura

Size From 1 in (2.5 cm) to 1.5 in (3.2 cm)

Key features Small; from above it appears teardrop shaped with a rounded body tapering to a pointed head; there is a distinctive fold of skin behind the head; limbs short; color gray or olive-green either without markings or with a few small, scattered dark spots

Habits Secretive; nocturnal; terrestrial

Breeding In flooded fields, ruts, and small pools; female lays very small eggs; tadpoles metamorphose after 30–50 days

Diet Small invertebrates, especially ants

Habitat Grasslands, open woods, and deserts

Distribution North America from Nebraska south to the Gulf Coast and across to Arizona, then into the lowlands of northern Mexico

Status Common

Similar species The eastern narrow-mouthed toad, *G. carolinensis,* has a more easterly distribution, although the 2 species overlap in parts of Texas and adjacent states; it is brown rather than gray in color and has a strongly patterned back

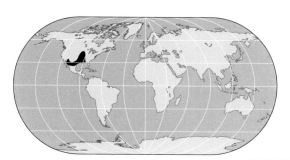

Darwin's Frog

Common name
Darwin's frog

Scientific name *Rhinoderma darwinii*

Family Rhinodermatidae

Order Anura

Size From 1 in (2.5 cm) to 1.2 in (3 cm)

Key features Body small and chubby; pointed snout ends in a short appendage; pupils horizontal; hind feet slightly webbed and have small flaps of skin on the ankles; bright green, brown, or reddish brown in color with faint spotting of darker hues; underneath is black with bright white spots and a gray throat

Habits Terrestrial; active by day; if alarmed, leaps into a nearby stream, often landing upside down and proceeds to feign death by drifting motionless

Breeding Female lays 30–40 eggs and abandons them; the male picks up the eggs and holds the developing tadpoles in his vocal sac

Diet Small invertebrates

Habitat Shallow cold streams running through southern beech forests

Distribution Southern Chile and adjacent parts of southern Argentina

Status Formerly common but becoming scarcer due to habitat reduction; listed as "Data Deficient" by the IUCN

Similar species *R. rufum* from the same region is similar

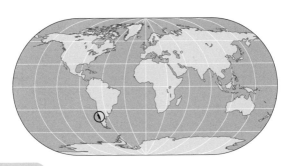

Seychelles Frogs

Gardiner's frog
(Sooglossus gardineri)

Common name
Seychelles frogs

Scientific name *Sooglossus* and *Nesomantis*

Family Sooglossidae

Order Anura

Number of Species 4 (Gardiner's frog, *S. gardineri*; palm frog, *S. pipilodryas*; Seychelles frog, *S. sechellensis*; Thomasset's rock frog, *Nesomantis thomasseti*)

Size From 0.4 in (10 mm) to 1.6 in (4 cm)

Key features Small, nondescript frogs; fingers and toes lack webbing; small, pointed toe pads; pupils horizontal; no external eardrums; color mostly brown on the back with darker flanks or irregular darker markings, making them difficult to see when resting among dead leaves on the forest floor

Habits Terrestrial; apparently active by day and night

Breeding Eggs hatch directly into small frogs or into nonfeeding tadpoles that complete their development on the female's back

Diet Small invertebrates

Habitat Moist forests, especially along ridges and among rocky outcrops where leaf litter accumulates

Distribution Mahé and Silhouette Islands, Seychelles

Status Gardiner's frog is the most common and widespread species;j the others are very uncommon

Similar species There are no other small brown frogs on the Seychelles Islands

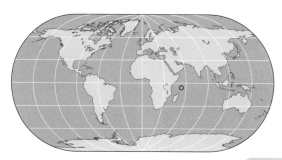

Reed Frogs

Spotted reed frog *(Hyperolius puncticulatus)*

Common name
Reed frogs, sedge frogs, bush frogs, leaf-folding frogs

Family Hyperoliidae

Order Anura

Number of species About 250 in 19 genera

Size From 0.6 in (17 mm) to 4.3 in (11 cm)

Key features Body usually slender with moderately long limbs; fingers and toes have expanded pads; pupils horizontally elliptical; color variable in shades of green or brown; many have bright yellow, red, or orange markings

Habits Mostly arboreal, some are terrestrial; nocturnal

Breeding Amplexus is axillary; eggs laid in water, on leaves, in foam nests on vegetation, or in holes on land near to water; fertilization external; eggs hatch into free-swimming tadpoles

Diet Invertebrates, including small insects and spiders

Habitat Varied from rain forest to savanna, grassland, and secondary forest or scrub

Distribution Sub-Saharan Africa, Madagascar, and Seychelles Islands

Status 3 species—Seychelles Islands treefrog, *Tachycnemis seychellensis*, Pickersgill's reed frog, *Hyperolius pickersgilli*, and the long-toed treefrog, *Leptopelis xenodactylus*—are Vulnerable (IUCN)

Similar species Treefrogs in the family Hylidae, but there is little or no overlap of families

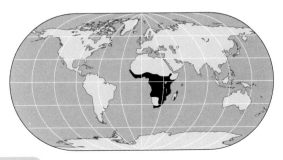

Ghost Frogs

Table Mountain ghost frog
(*Heleophryne rosei*)

Common name Ghost frogs

Scientific name *Heleophryne* sp.

Family Heleophrynidae

Order Anura

Number of Species 5 (Table Mountain ghost frog, *H. rosei*;
Natal ghost frog, *H. natalensis*; Cape ghost frog,
H. purcelli; Hewitt's ghost frog, *H. hewitti*)

Size From 1.2 in (3 cm) to 2.5 in (6.5 cm); the Natal ghost
frog is the largest species

Key features Body and head flattened for squeezing into cracks;
limbs long; tips of toes have adhesive pads for climbing
wet rocks; toes of the hind limbs are extensively webbed
for swimming; coloration varies among the species; 3 are
tan with darker markings, 1 is dark brown with yellow
markings, and the other is green with reddish-brown
markings

Habits Nocturnal; they climb among wet boulders and are
good swimmers

Breeding Takes place in streams; eggs are laid under rocks
and stones

Diet Invertebrates

Habitat Fast-flowing streams, cascades, and waterfalls in
mountainous places

Distribution Southern Africa; each species has a very restricted
range, 4 in the southern Cape region, and 1 in the
Natal Drakensberg

Status Rare; Hewitt's ghost frog is classed as Endangered,
and the Table Mountain ghost frog as Vulnerable by
the IUCN

Similar species None

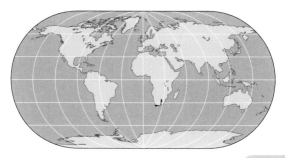

Valerio's Glass Frog

Common name
Valerio's glass
frog (La Palma
glass frog, reticulated glass frog)

Scientific name *Hyalinobatrachium valerioi*

Family Centrolenidae

Order Anura

Size From 0.75 in (2 cm) to 1 in (2.5 cm)

Key features Small, delicate body; eyes large; toes have
adhesive tips; internal organs can be seen when viewed
from the underside, hence the common name of "glass
frog"; body green with distinctive pale round markings
on darker green back

Habits Nocturnal; tree dwelling

Breeding Breeds alongside forest streams; female lays 30–40
eggs on leaves overhanging the water

Diet Small invertebrates, such as flies

Habitat Forest streams running through lowland and montane
rain forests

Distribution Central and South America (Central Costa Rica to
the western slopes of the Andes in Colombia)

Status Widespread and probably quite common in
undisturbed habitat

Similar species Most other members of the family are
superficially similar in appearance and habits, but the
round, pale spots are usually enough to distinguish it
from related species

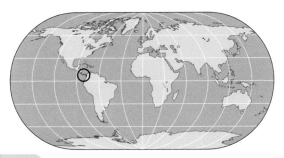

Casque-Headed Frogs

Hemiphractus scutatus

Common name Casque-headed frogs

Scientific name *Hemiphractus* sp.

Subfamily Hemiphractinae

Family Hylidae

Order Anura

Number of species 6 (*H. scutatus, H. helioi, H. johnsoni, H. fasciata, H. proboscideus, H. bubalis*)

Size From 1.6 in (4 cm) to 2.5 in (6.3 cm)

Key features Head and front part of body covered by a huge triangular, bony, helmetlike plate; plate narrows to a point at the tip of the snout and at the angle of the jaw on either side; all species are basically brown in color with lighter and darker mottled and reticulated markings; toe pads expanded in 5 species but lacking in the terrestrial species, *H. scutatus*

Habits Arboreal, semiarboreal, and terrestrial; strictly nocturnal

Breeding Females lay clutches of 2–14 large eggs; eggs carried on their backs in an exposed position

Diet Other frogs, small lizards, and invertebrates

Habitat Primary lowland forests and cloud forests from 825 ft (250 m) to 6,300 ft (1,920 m)

Distribution Central and South America (Panama to upper Amazon Basin)

Status Extremely rare or probably just hard to find

Similar species None

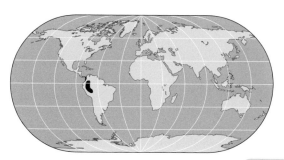

Riobamba Marsupial Frog

Common name
Riobamba marsupial frog

Scientific name *Gastrotheca riobambae*

Subfamily Hemiphractinae

Family Hylidae

Order Anura

Size From 1.5 in (4 cm) to 2.5 in (6 cm)

Key features Body plump (for a treefrog); head wide; snout blunt; the skin on its back is warty with a raised ridge running down either side; color can be uniform green or green with brown or bronze patches; insides of the thighs are often blue; toes long with fairly small pads

Habits Terrestrial; active in the evening

Breeding Female lays clutches of up to 100 eggs that she carries in a pouch on her back; tadpoles develop after 3–4 months

Diet Small invertebrates

Habitat A montane species living in a wide range of habitats, including fields

Distribution Andes of Ecuador and southern Colombia

Status Common

Similar species Several other marsupial frogs live in the Andes; they often go under the name of *G. marsupiata*, but this is just one of a number of quite similar species

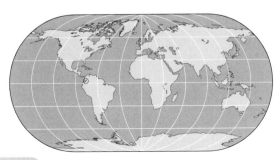

Common European Treefrog

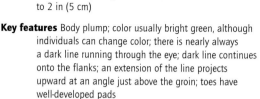

Common name Common European treefrog (green treefrog)

Scientific name *Hyla arborea*

Subfamily Hylinae

Family Hylidae

Order Anura

Size From 1.25 in (3 cm) to 2 in (5 cm)

Key features Body plump; color usually bright green, although individuals can change color; there is nearly always a dark line running through the eye; dark line continues onto the flanks; an extension of the line projects upward at an angle just above the groin; toes have well-developed pads

Habits Mainly nocturnal but diurnal on humid or rainy days; arboreal

Breeding Throughout the summer in shallow water; female lays clutches of 200–1,400 eggs; eggs hatch after 14–21 days

Diet Insects, especially flies

Habitat Heavily vegetated areas near water, such as reed beds, hedges, bushes, and trees

Distribution Throughout most of Europe except the British Isles, parts of southern France, southern and eastern Iberia; also into Asiatic Turkey and through the former Soviet states as far as the Caspian Sea

Status Very common in places

Similar species There are many closely related species, each occurring where the others do not—their ranges only rarely overlap

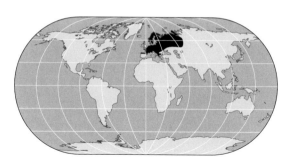

American Green Treefrog

Common name
American green treefrog (rain frog)

Scientific name *Hyla cinerea*

Subfamily Hylinae

Family Hylidae

Order Anura

Size From 1.25 in (3 cm) to 2.5 in (6 cm)

Key features Body slender; eyes golden; skin slightly granular; color bright green with a thick, creamy-white stripe running around the upper lips and extending down each side of the face and onto the flanks; some individuals may lack the side stripe, especially in the north of its range; a few scattered cream or golden spots often present on its back; hind legs longer than those of most treefrogs

Habits Arboreal; nocturnal

Breeding In ponds and the edges of lakes and backwaters; eggs laid in small clumps attached to aquatic vegetation

Diet Insects, especially flying species

Habitat In wetlands, in reed beds, palms, Spanish moss, and on large leaves

Distribution Southeastern United States

Status Very common in places

Similar species None in the area; the squirrel treefrog, *H. squirella*, is sometimes green but has a plumper shape and lacks the side stripe

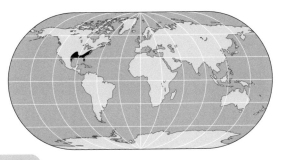

Cuban Treefrog

Common name Cuban treefrog (giant treefrog)

Scientific name *Osteopilus septentrionalis*

Subfamily Hylinae

Family Hylidae

Order Anura

Size From 2 in (5 cm) to 4.9 in (12.5 cm)

Key features Body large; skin slightly warty; usually light brown or buff in color, but some have extensive areas of green; irregular, darker patches often present on the back as well as bars on the hind legs; head flat and bony; toe pads conspicuous; female is considerably larger than the male

Habits Nocturnal; arboreal

Breeding In pools and cisterns; female lays clutches of 130 large eggs in floating rafts; eggs hatch after 2 days

Diet Large insects; other frogs

Habitat Often common around houses, in plant pots, drainpipes, and outhouses; also found in leaf axils of palms and other plants

Distribution Cuba (including the Isla de Juventud), Cayman Islands, and Bahamas; introduced to Puerto Rico, Virgin Islands, Anguilla, and southern Florida

Status Extremely common

Similar species Large body size, toe pads, and warty skin make adults unmistakable; juveniles may look like a number of other smaller, mostly brown treefrogs

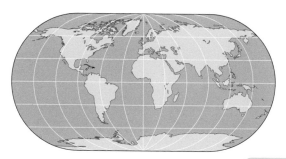

Australian Water-Holding Frog

Common name Australian water-holding frog (giant frog)

Scientific name *Cyclorana australis*

Subfamily Pelodryadinae

Family Hylidae

Order Anura

Size From 2.75 in (7 cm) to 4 in (10 cm)

Key features Body large, stocky, and muscular; color may be buff or pale brown, often marked with green; a pair of glandular ridges runs down either side of its back; another pair is present on its flanks; a wide dark "mask" crosses the eye and reaches the angle of the jaw; hind limbs long; hind feet have bony "spades"; extended toe pads lacking

Habits Nocturnal; terrestrial

Breeding In shallow temporary ponds; female lays thousands of eggs

Diet Other frogs and large invertebrates such as beetles and grasshoppers

Habitat Open areas often near water but also in dry places

Distribution North Australia from the Kimberley region (Western Australia) across the Northern Territory to northern Queensland

Status Common in suitable habitat

Similar species There are several similar *Cyclorana* species, including the New Holland frog, *C. novaehollandiae* (with which this species is often confused), another water-holding frog, *C. platycephala*, and the long-footed frog, *C. longipes*

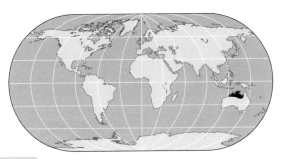

White's Treefrog

Common name
White's treefrog (green treefrog)

Scientific name *Litoria caerulea*

Subfamily Pelodryadinae

Family Hylidae

Order Anura

Size From 2 in (5 cm) to 4 in (10 cm); exceptionally to 5.5 in (14 cm)

Key features Body stocky; limbs and digits thick; skin smooth and appears slightly waxy; in nature its color is normally bright grass-green, but captive animals are often bluish green or gray; small cream-colored spots sometimes present on its back; toe pads very large and sticky; it appears to have a permanent grin; prominent fold of skin present above the eardrum

Habits Arboreal; nocturnal

Breeding Mating and egg laying take place in water; females lay up to 2,000 small eggs; eggs hatch after 1–2 days; tadpoles metamorphose in 4–5 weeks

Diet Large invertebrates, especially flying insects, and occasional small vertebrates such as lizards, other frogs, snakes, and rodents

Habitat Rain forests, drier, open woodland, and around human dwellings

Distribution Northeastern Australia and southern New Guinea

Status Common

Similar species There are a number of other large green treefrogs in the region, but none are as common

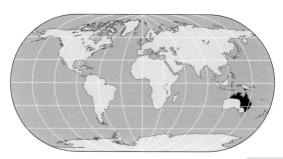

Red-Eyed Leaf Frogs

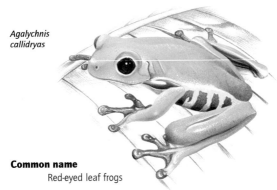

Agalychnis callidryas

Common name
Red-eyed leaf frogs

Scientific name *Agalychnis callidryas* and *A. saltator*

Subfamily Phyllomedusinae

Family Hylidae

Order Anura

Size *A. callidryas:* 2.8 in (7 cm); *A. saltator:* 2.4 in (6 cm)

Key features Body slender; waist narrow; legs long and spindly; feet webbed; toes have expanded sticky pads; eyes very large with brilliant-red irises; pupils vertical, separating them from all other treefrogs except other members of the Phyllomedusinae; *A. callidryas* has blue-and-cream markings on its flanks, varying according to location

Habits Highly arboreal; mostly nocturnal

Breeding Eggs laid on leaves overhanging small pools; on average female lays 29–51 eggs, possibly in several clutches; eggs hatch after 5 days (*A. callidryas*); 21–72 eggs that hatch after about 6 days (*A. saltator*)

Diet Invertebrates

Habitat Lowland rain forests

Distribution Central America from southern Veracruz and the Yucatán Peninsula, Mexico, to the Canal Zone, Panama (*A. callidryas*); *A. saltator* has a more restricted range from northeastern Nicaragua to northeastern Costa Rica

Status Common in suitable habitat but declining

Similar species Several other *Agalychnis* species occur in the region but none with bright red eyes

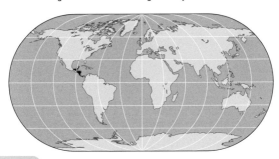

Strawberry Poison Dart Frog

Common name Strawberry poison dart frog (strawberry frog)

Scientific name *Dendrobates pumilio*

Family Dendrobatidae

Order Anura

Size From 0.7 in (1.8 cm) to 1 in (2.5 cm)

Key features Body small but quite plump; snout short and blunt; eyes large and black; limbs thin; in its most common color form the head and body are bright strawberry-red or orange-red; back legs and lower parts of the front legs are black or dark blue; sometimes small dark-blue or black spots occur on the back; males have a buff-colored patch on the throat; bright colors indicate presence of poison glands in skin that secrete batrachotoxin, one of the stongest nerve poisons in the animal world; can be lethal

Habits Diurnal; terrestrial

Breeding Mating and egg laying take place on the ground; female lays several clutches of up to 5 eggs; eggs hatch after 7 days; female feeds tadpoles with infertile eggs

Diet Small invertebrates, especially ants and forest mites

Habitat Lowland rain forests, including some secondary forests and clearings

Distribution Central America on the Atlantic watersheds of eastern Nicaragua, Costa Rica, and northern Panama

Status Very numerous in suitable habitats

Similar species 2 similar species, both predominantly red: *D. granuliferus* (but it has a granular back, while *D. pumilio* has a smooth back) and *D. speciosus*, which is red all over; other red species occur in South America

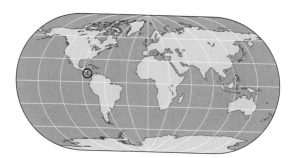

Orange Poison Dart Frog

Common name Orange poison dart frog (terrible poison dart frog)

Scientific name *Phyllobates terribilis*

Family Dendrobatidae

Order Anura

Size 1.6 in (4 cm)

Key features Completely orange-yellow in color with a metallic texture; there is also a "green" form that is metallic bronzy-green; eyes black; limbs slender, as in most species; toe pads very small, barely noticeable; glands in the skin produce a powerful neurotoxin capable of causing death even in humans if it enters victim's bloodstream

Habits Diurnal; terrestrial

Breeding Takes place on the ground; female lays about 20 eggs; eggs hatch after about 5 days

Diet Small invertebrates, especially ants

Habitat Primary lowland rain forests at about 300 ft (91 m) to 600 ft (182 m) elevation

Distribution Department of Cauca, Colombia

Status Apparently common within its small range

Similar species The black-legged poison dart frog, *P. bicolor*, is similar, but its feet and the lower parts of its limbs are black; it also has black markings along the flanks and on the lower parts of its face

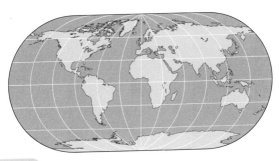

American Bullfrog

Common name American bullfrog

Scientific name *Rana catesbeiana*

Subfamily Raninae

Family Ranidae

Order Anura

Size From 3.5 in (9 cm) to 8 in (20 cm); when stretched out, it can measure 36 in (91 cm)

Key features A large frog (the largest in North America) with long, powerful hind legs and heavily webbed feet; eardrum prominent and larger in male than in female; color mottled olive, brown, or green above and lighter green on the head; legs are banded or spotted with dark brown or black; chin and throat also have dark markings; its bellowing call is loud and distinctive

Habits Semiaquatic, rarely seen far from water

Breeding Female lays masses of spawn in water in spring and summer; eggs hatch after 4 days

Diet Large invertebrates and small vertebrates, including other frogs

Habitat Large ponds and lakes; usually stays near the water's edge or rests among floating vegetation

Distribution Eastern and central North America; introduced to western United States and other regions

Status Common

Similar species Adults are distinctive on account of their size; juveniles could be confused with several other medium-sized ranids from the region

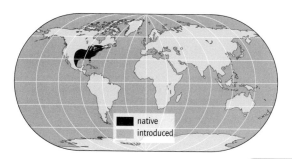

native
introduced

Common Frog

Common name Common frog (grass frog)

Scientific name *Rana temporaria*

Subfamily Raninae

Family Ranidae

Order Anura

Size From 2 in (5 cm) to 4 in (10 cm)

Key features Very variable; brown, greenish, pinkish, yellowish, or tan in color with dark "mask" markings behind the eyes; back legs have dark bars across them; adults have a rounded snout, but juveniles have a more streamlined shape; skin smooth except for a pair of raised fleshy ridges running down either side of its back

Habits Diurnal and nocturnal; terrestrial

Breeding Mating and egg laying take place in water in the spring with large masses of spawn; females lay 700–4,500 eggs; eggs hatch after 7–40 days depending on temperature

Diet Invertebrates, including slugs and insects

Habitat Highly varied; woods, hedges, bogs, fields, meadows, ditches, ponds, streams, and sluggish rivers

Distribution Central and northern Europe eastward across Siberia

Status The commonest frog over much of its range

Similar species Similar to several other frogs in the region, especially the agile frog, *R. dalmatina*, and several North American species, notably the wood frog, *R. sylvatica*

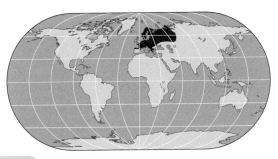

Edible Frog

Common name Edible frog

Scientific name *Rana kl. esculenta*

Subfamily Raninae

Family Ranidae

Order Anura

Size 4.7 in (12 cm)

Key features Body plump compared to other ranids; head triangular; snout pointed; hind legs are muscular but not obviously long as in some species; usually green in color with a lighter stripe running down the center of the back; back of the thighs are often yellow; a low fleshy ridge runs down each side of its back; back feet have a horny "spade"

Habits Very aquatic, can even feed underwater; active at night and during the day

Breeding Female lays large numbers of eggs in water

Diet Invertebrates

Habitat Almost any body of water from small, muddy pools, ditches, canals, and ponds to the edges of lakes; also found in brackish water

Distribution Central and eastern Europe; small colonies in southern England may be introduced

Status Common in suitable habitats

Similar species The two parent species (from which the hybrid edible frog is produced), the marsh frog, *R. ridibunda*, and the pool frog, *R. lessonae*, are very similar

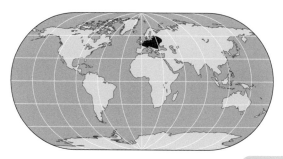

Giant African Bullfrog

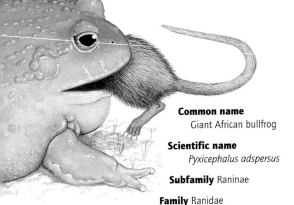

Common name
Giant African bullfrog

Scientific name
Pyxicephalus adspersus

Subfamily Raninae

Family Ranidae

Order Anura

Size From 3.5 in (9 cm) to 9 in (23 cm)

Key features Adults massive, almost as wide as they are long; body flaccid; legs short; head is proportionately large, and they have a huge gape; 2 razor-sharp tusks, or "false teeth," present on the lower jaw; skin mostly smooth but with a number of raised fleshy ridges along the back; adults are dull green in color with yellow areas at the base of their limbs, brighter in breeding males; juveniles are mottled green and buff with a pale line running down the center of the back; males grow larger than females

Habits Burrowing; mainly nocturnal

Breeding In shallow, temporary pools; clutches of eggs laid together in a small area

Diet Smaller frogs, small mammals, lizards, snakes, and large insects

Habitat Open savanna and scrub

Distribution Much of Africa south of the Sahara in suitable habitat

Status Common in places but often not seen for long periods between breeding seasons

Similar species The African bullfrog, *P. edulis*; the 2 species used to be grouped together but are now recognized as different

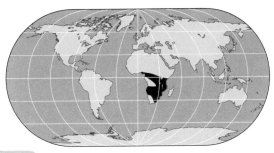

African Foam-Nesting Treefrog

Common name African foam-nesting treefrog (gray treefrog)

Scientific name *Chiromantis xerampelina*

Subfamily Rhacophorinae

Family Rhacophoridae

Order Anura

Size From 2.75 in (7 cm) to 3.3 in (8.4 cm)

Key features Body stocky; eyes large; pupils horizontally elliptical; hands and feet webbed; toe pads large and sticky; toes opposable, allowing it to grip thin twigs; back is rough textured, usually gray, but can be almost white or brown with darker markings even in the same animal; females are larger than males

Habits Arboreal; active at night; rests in exposed positions in the day

Breeding Female lays 500–1,200 eggs in foam nests; eggs hatch after 3–5 days

Diet Invertebrates

Habitat Wooded grasslands, including seasonally dry areas

Distribution Southern and East Africa; an apparently isolated population occurs in Angola

Status Common

Similar species 3 other species of *Chiromantis* in Africa, but none of them occurs with this species

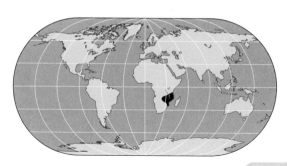

Reinwardt's Flying Frog

Common name Reinwardt's flying frog

Scientific name *Rhacophorus reinwardtii*

Subfamily Rhacophorinae

Family Rhacophoridae

Order Anura

Size From 1.8 in (4.6 cm) to 2.6 in (6.6 cm)

Key features Medium size; head wide; eyes large; pupils horizontal; hands and feet very large and all completely webbed; toe pads large and sticky; forearms have a fringe of loose skin; lower legs have flaps of skin; color bright or dark green and sometimes yellow on the flanks; webbing between the toes is yellow and blue or black and blue; females tend to be bigger than males

Habits Arboreal; nocturnal

Breeding Eggs laid in a foam nest; eggs hatch into pond-type tadpoles

Diet Insects

Habitat Primary rain forests at low elevations

Distribution Southeast Asia (Malaysian Peninsula, Sumatra, Java, and Borneo)

Status Probably common in suitable habitat but hard to observe

Similar species Several other *Rhacophorus* species from the region are green and of a similar size

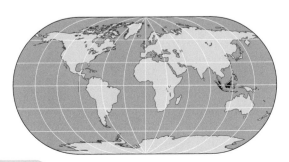

Bush Frogs

Philautus gracilipes

Common name
Bush frogs

Scientific name
Philautus sp.

Subfamily Rhacophorinae

Family Rhacophoridae

Order Anura

Number of species About 85

Size Up to about 1.6 in (4 cm)

Key features Small, stocky frogs with toe pads; eyes large and bulging; pupils horizontal; most species have smooth skin, but some have slightly warty or wrinkled skin; a few have a narrow frill of skin along the edges of their limbs to help break up their outline; brown or green in color; many species are highly variable

Habits Arboreal; strictly nocturnal

Breeding A variety of egg-laying sites used; some species probably have direct development

Diet Small invertebrates

Habitat Hill forests up to 9,800 ft (3,000 m) on Mount Kinabalu, Borneo, but lower elsewhere; a few species found at sea level

Distribution Southern India, Sri Lanka, and Southeast Asia

Status Common in suitable habitat but poorly studied

Similar species There are other small rhacophorids in the region

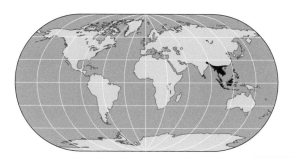

Mantellas

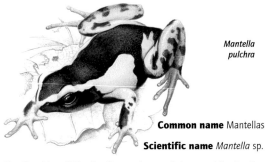

*Mantella
pulchra*

Common name Mantellas

Scientific name *Mantella* sp.

Family Mantellidae (until recently regarded as a subfamily of Rhacophoridae)

Order Anura

Number of species 12 named species and several awaiting description

Size From 0.8 in (20 mm) to 1.2 in (3 cm)

Key features Colorful, lively frogs; skin smooth or slightly granular; some are uniform orange, others are black with patches of various bold colors, such as orange, yellow, red, green, and even blue in a few cases; the green-backed mantella, *M. laevigata*, is the only member of the genus with expanded toe pads

Habits Diurnal; mostly terrestrial, but *M. laevigata* climbs into low bushes and trees

Breeding Females lay small clutches of eggs on the ground or in tree holes; tadpoles hatch after about 7–14 days and then find their way to water

Diet Small invertebrates, including ants

Habitat Tropical rain forests

Distribution Madagascar

Status Some species have very small ranges, but they often occur in high densities; habitat destruction has reduced the distribution of several species

Similar species None in the region, but their convergence with the poison dart frogs, *Dendrobates* species from Central and South America, is remarkable

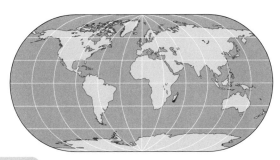

Loggerhead Turtle

Common name Loggerhead turtle

Scientific name *Caretta caretta*

Family Cheloniidae

Suborder Cryptodira

Order Testudines

Size Carapace 41 in (104 cm) long

Weight Up to 1,200 lb (544 kg)

Key features Very big head and powerful jaws; carapace heart shaped, lacking ridges in adult (but juvenile's carapace is ridged); carapace brown, often with light brown, reddish-brown, or black markings; plastron yellowish-brown in color; limbs paddlelike and have 2 claws on each

Habits Tends to breed farther from the equator than many turtles; relatively aggressive

Breeding Nesting interval typically 2–3 years but can range from 1–6 years; females come ashore to lay clutches of 100 eggs 4–7 times during the breeding season; eggs hatch after 54–68 days

Diet Mainly shellfish, including mussels, clams, and crabs; may eat some seaweed

Habitat Coastal areas, often in relatively shallow water; occurs in muddy waters as well as clear tropical seas

Distribution Wide range through the Pacific, Indian, and Atlantic Oceans, especially in southeastern United States; occurs as far north as Newfoundland and as far south as Argentina

Status Endangered (IUCN); listed on CITES Appendix I

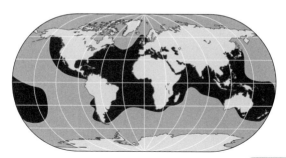

Green Turtle

Common name Green turtle

Scientific name *Chelonia mydas*

Family Cheloniidae

Suborder Cryptodira

Order Testudines

Size Carapace usually over 36 in (91 cm) long

Weight Up to 352 lb (160 kg) when adult

Key features Head relatively small with prominent pair of scales in front of eyes; jaw serrated along its edges; distinctive differences in appearance between Atlantic and Pacific populations, the latter having a significantly darker plastron; carapace dome shaped: black, gray, brown, often greenish due to underlying fat; limbs paddlelike, usually with a single claw on each one

Habits A marine turtle occurring in coastal areas rather than roaming across the open ocean; some populations bask during the day

Breeding Female lays about 115 eggs per clutch on average 3–5 times during a season; interval between laying is usually 2–3 years; eggs hatch after about 65 days

Diet Small individuals feed on small crustaceans and similar creatures; larger individuals are entirely herbivorous, eating sea grass and marine algae

Habitat Coastal areas, bays, and shallow water in tropical and temperate seas

Distribution Pacific and Atlantic Oceans

Status Endangered (IUCN); listed on CITES Appendix I

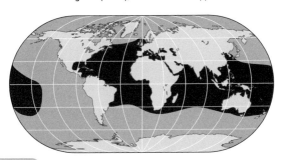

Hawksbill Turtle

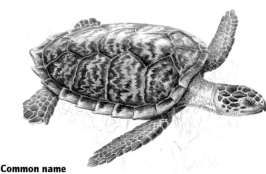

Common name
    Hawksbill turtle

Scientific name *Eretmochelys imbricata*

Family Cheloniidae

Suborder Cryptodira

Order Testudines

Size Carapace up to 36 in (91 cm) long

Weight Up to 150 lb (68 kg)

Key features Head narrow and distinctive with a hawklike bill;
2 pairs of scales in front of the eyes; carapace elliptical
with an attractive blend of yellow or orange mixed with
brown, but coloration is highly individual; scutes overlap
behind each other on the carapace; 2 claws present on
each flipper; serrations present on side of carapace

Habits Often encountered looking for prey on coral reefs

Breeding Female usually lays up to 160 eggs in a season but
breeds on average only every 2–4 years; eggs hatch after
58–75 days

Diet Invertebrates, mainly sponges, but also squid and shrimp

Habitat Mainly tropical waters

Distribution Occurs in the Atlantic and in parts of the Indian
and Pacific oceans

Status Endangered (IUCN); listed on CITES Appendix I

Leatherback Turtle

Common name
Leatherback turtle

Scientific name *Dermochelys coriacea*

Family Dermochelyidae

Suborder Cryptodira

Order Testudines

Size Carapace can grow to 8 ft (2.4 m) long

Weight Up to 1,650 lb (750 kg)

Key features Carapace very distinctive with 7 ridges running down its length; surface of the carapace is effectively a rubbery skin rather than made up of scales; skin strengthened with very small bony plates; color dark with whitish markings; plastron bears about 5 ridges and varies in color from a whitish shade to black; flippers lack claws; front flippers extremely long; carapace of hatchlings has rows of white scales

Habits Often favors open sea, swimming widely through the world's oceans

Breeding Clutches consist of about 80 viable eggs; female typically produces 6-9 clutches per season; egg-laying interval typically 2-3 years; youngsters emerge after about 65 days

Diet Almost exclusively jellyfish

Habitat Temperate and tropical waters

Distribution Has the largest range of any marine turtle; found in all the world's oceans from Alaska to New Zealand

Status Critically Endangered (IUCN); listed on CITES Appendix I

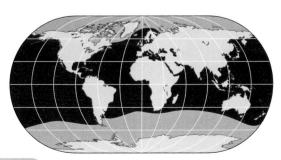

Oblong Snake-Necked Turtle

Common name Oblong snake-necked turtle

Scientific name *Chelodina oblonga*

Family Chelidae

Suborder Pleurodira

Order Testudines

Size Carapace at least 12.3 in (31 cm); up to 15.8 in (40 cm) according to some reports

Weight Approximately 3.3 lb (1.5 kg)

Key features Carapace has an oblong outline; neck when extended is virtually as long as the body and very muscular; color of the carapace very variable, ranging from dark fawn through blue-gray to black, occasionally dark brown with speckling; plastron bone-colored to brown; up to 12 tiny barbels (sensory projections) present under the chin; neck has a warty appearance; a dark band runs through the eyes; males tend to be slightly longer with a more concave plastron and a cloacal opening positioned farther back along the tail from the body

Habits Predatory by nature; sometimes wanders into gardens to nest

Breeding Female lays up to 156 eggs per clutch up to 3 times a year; eggs hatch after 30 weeks

Diet Carnivorous, hunting various invertebrates, amphibians, and fish; may also take small birds

Habitat Relatively slow-flowing rivers, lakes, and similar aquatic areas

Disribution Southwestern Australia

Status Does not appear under threat

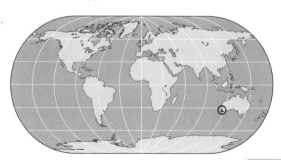

Matamata

Common name Matamata

Scientific name *Chelus fimbriatus*

Family Chelidae

Suborder Pleurodira

Order Testudines

Size Carapace 18 in (46 cm) long

Weight 33 lb (15 kg)

Key features Head very broad, flat, and triangular when seen from above; conspicuous skin flaps on head for detecting prey; nostrils protrude at the end of narrow tubes on the snout; eyes very small and positioned on top of the head; head coloration chestnut-brown above; throat reddish in hatchlings but variable in color in adults; young matamatas have a chestnut-red carapace, which is darker (almost black) in some adults; red plastron becomes brownish with age; small feet show little webbing; scales separated by areas of rough skin are evident on the limbs; tail short and tapering to a point

Habits Sedentary; hunts by ambush; almost entirely aquatic but not a powerful swimmer

Breeding Female lays clutch of about 20 almost spherical eggs with hard, calcareous shells; eggs can take about 30 weeks to hatch

Diet Small fish; possibly also crustaceans

Habitat Prefers calm waters such as lakes and ponds

Distribution Northern South America; widely distributed in suitable habitat throughout the Amazon basin

Status Not presumed endangered nor subject to heavy hunting pressure

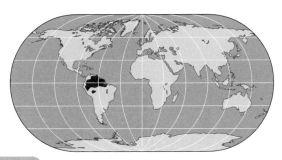

Krefft's River Turtle

Common name Krefft's river turtle

Scientific name *Emydura krefftii*

Family Chelidae

Suborder Pleurodira

Order Testudines

Size Carapace up to 13.5 in (34 cm) long

Weight Approximately 2.75 lb (1.25 kg)

Key features Appearance varies across its range; head larger in some populations than others; a distinctive facial stripe extends back on each side of the head from the eye to the rounded area of skin at the side (which is the tympanum); a narrow, bright yellow ring is present around the pupil; iris is greenish in some populations; there are tiny swellings near the neck, but the head is covered in smooth, gray skin; carapace is dark, varying from shades of olive-green through brown to blackish in some cases

Habits Fairly sedentary; can be seen basking on riverbanks; may travel short distances overland

Breeding Female typically lays 3 clutches at monthly intervals, each with about 16 eggs; eggs hatch after about 7–10 weeks

Diet Omnivorous; eats animal and vegetable matter, including fruit and crustaceans

Habitat Mostly river and drainage systems; not usually encountered in fast-flowing waters

Distribution Northeastern Australia ranging from Princess Charlotte Bay as far south as Brisbane

Status Does not appear under threat

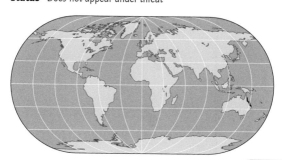

Pan-Hinged Terrapin

Common name Pan-hinged terrapin
(East African black mud turtle)

Scientific name *Pelusios subniger*

Family Pelomedusidae

Suborder Pleurodira

Order Testudines

Size Carapace up to 8 in (20 cm) in length

Weight Approximately 18 lb (0.8 kg)

Key features Shell relatively flat, smooth, and oval; body and head brownish to match shell; plastron hinged at the front; head large and brownish, occasionally marked with black spots; a pair of barbels normally present under the chin

Habits Nocturnal; more likely to be active during the day in the rainy season

Breeding Female lays about 8 eggs per clutch, possibly several times in the late summer; eggs usually hatch after 15 weeks

Diet Omnivorous; eats plant and animal matter

Habitat Stagnant areas of standing water such as ponds; sometimes found in sluggish streams

Distribution Tanzania and Burundi in East Africa southward to parts of the Democratic Republic of Congo, Botswana, and Zambia; found as far south as Mozambique and Kruger National Park, South Africa; also present on islands off the east coast, notably Madagascar, Seychelles, and Mauritius

Status Does not appear endangered

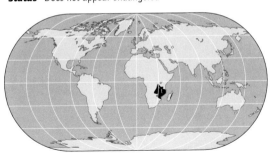

Yellow-Spotted River Turtle

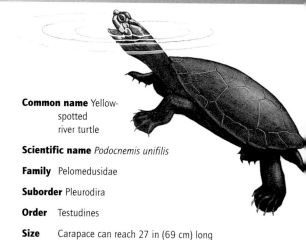

Common name Yellow-spotted river turtle

Scientific name *Podocnemis unifilis*

Family Pelomedusidae

Suborder Pleurodira

Order Testudines

Size Carapace can reach 27 in (69 cm) long

Weight 20 lb (9 kg)

Key features Carapace has a convex shape most apparent in juveniles; 2nd and 3rd vertebral scutes slightly keeled; color ranges from dark brown to black; yellow to orange spots on head; front lobe of the plastron is shorter and wider than the rear lobe, and is a lighter buff-gray color in juveniles but grayer in adults (often with black markings); irises in females are blackish but green in males and juveniles; adult females also differ from males by a lack of head spots; those in males disappear by the time they reach maturity; females generally grow to a larger overall size

Habits Highly aquatic but may occasionally bask, typically in groups

Breeding Females lay 15–40 eggs in a clutch depending on location; eggs hatch after 63 days

Diet Predominantly, but not exclusively, herbivorous; eats aquatic plants and snails

Habitat Rivers, lakes; avoids fast-flowing water

Distribution Colombia eastward throughout the Amazon basin, including the Orinoco, extending as far south as parts of Bolivia and Brazil

Status Vulnerable (IUCN) because of hunting pressure

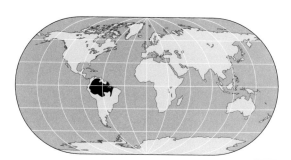

Alligator Snapping Turtle

Common name Alligator snapping turtle

Scientific name *Macroclemys temminckii*

Family Chelydridae

Suborder Cryptodira

Order Testudines

Size Carapace length about 26 in (66 cm)

Weight 219 lb (99.5 kg)

Key features Head large; jaws prominent and hooked; tail long; carapace varies in color from brown to gray depending on the individual and has 3 distinctive keels arranged in ridges, resembling those on the back of an alligator; feet on all four limbs end in sharp claws; lure present in mouth to attract prey

Habits Sedentary predator usually found in deep stretches of water; lures prey within reach especially during the daytime; may become more active as a hunter at night; strictly aquatic, but females leave the water to lay their eggs; relatively weak swimmer

Breeding Occurs in spring and early summer; clutches contain up to 50 eggs that hatch after about 100 days

Diet Eats anything it can catch, including birds, small mammals, other turtles, fish, and mussels where available; also eats fruit and nuts

Habitat Relatively sluggish stretches of water

Distribution North America from Kansas, Illinois, and Indiana to the Gulf of Mexico, including Florida and eastern Texas

Status Declining; now rare in many parts of its range; protected locally in parts of United States; Vulnerable (IUCN)

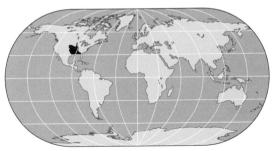

Common Snapping Turtle

Common name
Common
snapping turtle

Scientific name *Chelydra serpentina*

Family Chelydridae

Suborder Cryptodira

Order Testudines

Size Carapace length up to 24 in (61 cm)

Weight Up to 82 lb (37.2 kg)

Key features Head powerful; jaw hooked; barbels present on lower jaw; small tubercles on the neck and underparts; eyes prominently located near the snout; carapace brown and relatively smooth in older individuals but with a more pronounced keel in younger turtles; plastron relatively small in area with no patterning and varies from whitish to coppery brown; tail quite long with a crest running down the upper surface

Habits Relatively shy; spends long periods concealed in mud or vegetation; usually more active at night; often rests during the day, floating just under the surface with the eyes protruding

Breeding Female lays 1 clutch of 25–80 eggs (but may lay more than once a year); eggs hatch after 2 months

Diet Predominantly carnivorous; eats fish, amphibians, other turtles, birds, snakes, and small mammals; also eats plant matter

Habitat Occurs in virtually any type of standing or flowing fresh water, especially where there is a muddy base and vegetation

Distribution Southern parts of Canada through the United States and Central America south to Ecuador

Status Reasonably common

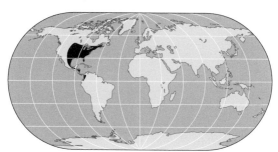

Big-Headed Turtle

Common name Big-headed turtle

Scientific name *Platysternon megacephalum*

Family Platysternidae

Suborder Cryptodira

Order Testudines

Size Carapace up to 8 in (20 cm) long

Weight Approximately 2.2 lb (1 kg)

Key features Head massive, its width sometimes half the length of the carapace; skull covered in a thick, bony casing; jaws powerful with a hook at the tip; top of head protected by a single horny scute extending down behind the eyes; carapace relatively flat and brownish with variable blackish markings and a central ridge running down its length; tail long, almost as long as the carapace when curled back; plastron light brown with a variable blackish patterning

Habits Nocturnal; very aggressive; can often be encountered on land as well as in water

Breeding Female lays small clutches of just 1 or 2 eggs; hatching time about 2–3 months

Diet Fish and various invertebrates; may venture onto land to feed

Habitat Fast-flowing mountain streams

Distribution Southeastern parts of Asia

Status Endangered (IUCN); listed on CITES Appendix II

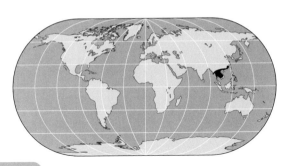

Pig-Nosed Turtle

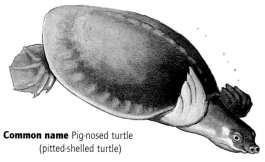

Common name Pig-nosed turtle
(pitted-shelled turtle)

Scientific name *Carettochelys insculpta*

Family Carettochelyidae

Suborder Cryptodira

Order Testudines

Size Carapace up to 22 in (56 cm) in the case of the New Guinea population

Weight Up to 50 lb (22.5 kg)

Key features Broad front flippers and paddlelike hind legs make it look like a sea turtle; number of claws is also reduced to 2 on each limb; snout highly distinctive and piglike, almost resembling a small trunk; thin skin covering the shell is pitted, accounting for its alternative common name of pitted-shelled turtle

Habits Highly aquatic; only females come onto land to breed; often remain still under water to avoid being seen

Breeding Australian females lay 7–19 eggs in a single clutch each year; eggs take at least 70 days to hatch

Diet Omnivorous; feeds on fruit such as figs, vegetation, and invertebrates such as crustaceans and mollusks

Habitat Relatively shallow, slow-flowing stretches of water

Distribution Southern New Guinea; Northern Territory in Australia

Status Has declined in some parts of New Guinea over recent years; Australian population appears stable; Vulnerable (IUCN)

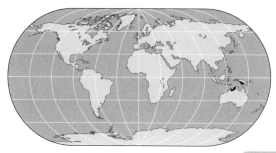

Spiny Softshell

Common name
Spiny softshell

Scientific name *Apalone spinifera*

Family Trionychidae

Suborder Cryptodira

Order Testudines

Size Carapace length 6.5 in (16.5 cm) to 18 in (46 cm) in females; from 5 in (13 cm) to 9.3 in (23.5 cm) in males

Weight Approximately 2.2 lb (1 kg) to 3.3 lb (1.5 kg)

Key features Flattened, leathery shell lacks scutes and is circular; underlying color varies from olive to tan; patterning highly variable; spots (ocelli) on carapace have black edges; distinctive spiny tubercles on the front edge of shell are unique to this species; neck long with dark-edged lighter stripes; nostrils elongated and snorkel-like; limbs powerful and paddlelike

Habits Fast swimmer; predominantly aquatic but will emerge to bask occasionally; burrows into mud or sand beneath the water to hide with just the head exposed

Breeding Female lays 4–32 white, spherical eggs; eggs probably hatch after about 8–10 weeks

Diet Carnivorous; eats mainly invertebrates such as crayfish; larger individuals may take fish and amphibians

Habitat Still or slow-flowing waters that are often shallow with a sandy or muddy bottom; may also occur in faster-flowing waters

Distribution North America from southern Canada south across the southern United States, including the Florida Peninsula, and around the Gulf Coast in Mexico

Status Generally quite common

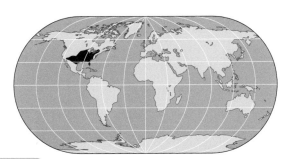

Central American River Turtle

Common name Central American river turtle

Scientific name *Dermatemys mawii*

Family Dermatemydidae

Suborder Cryptodira

Order Testudines

Size Carapace length up to 26 in (66 cm)

Weight Up to 48.5 lb (22 kg)

Key features Carapace flattish, olive-green in color with a thin covering of scutes that are easily damaged but with a well-developed bony skeleton beneath; feet powerful and webbed to aid swimming; head small relative to largish body size

Habits Highly aquatic; spends much of the time floating near the surface of the water

Breeding Female may lay 2 clutches a year averaging 6–20 eggs

Diet Mainly herbivorous; eats fruit and aquatic plants

Habitat Found in rivers and also calmer, large areas of water including lakes and lagoons

Distribution Central America from the Atlantic lowland region of southern Mexico (Veracruz, Campeche, Chiapas) into northern parts of Guatemala and Belize; an isolated population in Honduras

Status Endangered (IUCN); protected locally

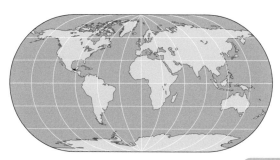

Yellow Mud Turtle

Common name Yellow mud turtle

Scientific name *Kinosternon flavescens*

Family Kinosternidae

Suborder Cryptodira

Order Testudines

Size Length of carapace 6.3 in (16 cm) maximum

Weight Approximately 1.3 lb (0.6 kg)

Key features Carapace predominantly olive-brown and smooth with an oval shape; yellow coloration confined largely to the jaw and throat area, including the 2 barbels on the chin; plastron relatively large and light brown in color (darker in some individuals than others) with distinct hinges at either end; males have a concave plastron and patches of scales on the inner side of the hind legs; tail long, ending in a spiny tip

Habits Spends daytime in water, often emerging to feed on land at night; most active during June and July

Breeding Female typically lays 1 clutch containing 4 eggs, but numbers vary from 1–6; eggs hatch after about 75 days

Diet Omnivorous; eats mainly aquatic invertebrates; on land eats snails and other terrestrial invertebrates

Habitat Slow-flowing streams and similar stretches of fresh water, especially where there is plenty of aquatic vegetation

Distribution Central and southern United States to Mexico

Status Reasonably common, although the subspecies *K. f. spooneri* is regarded as State Endangered in Illinois, Iowa, and Missouri

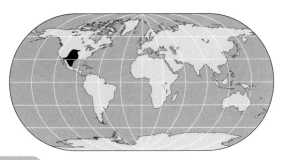

Painted Turtle

Common name Painted turtle

Scientific name *Chrysemys picta*

Family Emydidae

Suborder Cryptodira

Order Testudines

Size Carapace length up to 10 in (25 cm)

Weight Approximately 2.2 lb (1 kg)

Key features Shell smooth with no keel or serrations along the
rear of the carapace; yellow stripes on head, becoming
reddish on the sides of head and front legs; in the
eastern painted turtle, *C. p. picta*, the central vertebral
shields and adjacent side shields are aligned rather than
overlapping; different subspecies identified by distinctive
coloring and patterning; females grow larger than males;
males have longer front claws than females

Habits Semiaquatic; often leaves the water to bask

Breeding Female may produce clutches of anything from 2-20
eggs; eggs hatch after 10-11 weeks on average

Diet Young tend to be carnivorous; mature painted turtles eat
a higher percentage of aquatic vegetation

Habitat Relatively tranquil stretches of water, ranging from
smaller streams to lakes and rivers; eastern form
occasionally found in brackish water

Distribution Central and eastern parts of North America from
Canada in the north to Mexico in the south

Status Relatively common

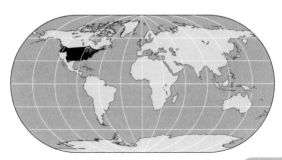

Pond Slider

Common name Pond slider

Scientific name *Chrysemys scripta*

Family Emydidae

Suborder Cryptodira

Order Testudines

Size Varies from 8.3 in (21 cm) to 24 in (60 cm) depending on subspecies; females always grow larger than males

Weight Approximately 2.2 lb (1 kg) to 4.4 lb (2 kg)

Key features Vary with subspecies; the well-known red-eared slider, *C. s. elegans*, has distinctive red flashes on either side of the head behind the eyes, which are pale green with a dark horizontal stripe; body has a striped pattern consisting of yellow and green markings; carapace greenish with darker markings, especially in older individuals; plastron yellowish with dark markings unique to each individual

Habits Semiaquatic; emerges regularly to bask

Breeding Female lays 12–15 eggs in a clutch, often nesting several times in a season; eggs hatch after 6–10 weeks on average

Diet Invertebrates, including tadpoles and aquatic snails; small fish; adults also eat plant matter

Habitat Slow-flowing stretches of water with plenty of vegetation

Distribution North, Central, and South America

Status Relatively common

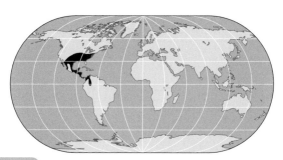

European Pond Turtle

Common name European pond turtle

Scientific name *Emys orbicularis*

Family Emydidae

Suborder Cryptodira

Order Testudines

Size Carapace length from 5 in (13 cm) to 7 in (18 cm)

Weight Approximately 1.8 lb (0.8 kg)

Key features Carapace relatively low and flattened; coloration varies but usually consists of a dark background with yellow markings in the form of streaks or spots; head coloration blackish with yellow spots; tail in males longer than in females; males also have a slightly concave plastron and red rather than yellow eyes; females larger on average than males

Habits Semiaquatic; will emerge to bask, but behavior varies throughout its wide range

Breeding Mating takes place under water; female lays clutch of 3-16 eggs (with an average of 9) on land; eggs usually hatch after about 70 days

Diet Aquatic invertebrates and fish; adults tend to eat more plant matter

Habitat Relatively sluggish stretches of water as well as ponds

Distribution Europe from Lithuania and Poland in the north across most of southern Europe and into North Africa and east to Turkmenistan

Status Declining in many areas because of pollution and habitat modification; Lower Risk (IUCN)

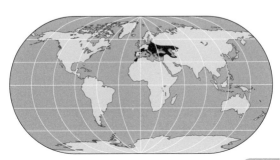

Eastern Box Turtle

Common name Eastern box turtle

Scientific name *Terrapene carolina*

Family Emydidae

Suborder Cryptodira

Order Testudines

Size Carapace length up to 8 in (20 cm)

Weight Approximately 2.2 lb (1 kg)

Key features Carapace relatively domed, usually brownish in color often with variable markings; body predominantly brown with yellow and orange markings particularly on the chin and front legs (depending to some extent on the subspecies and the individual); plastron relatively plain with distinctive hinged flaps front and back, allowing the turtle to seal itself into its shell completely; males generally have reddish irises, but those of females are brownish

Habits Spends much of its time on land but usually remains close to water; may immerse itself for long periods, especially during dry spells

Breeding Female lays 3-8 eggs in a clutch, sometimes more than once in a season; eggs hatch after 9-18 weeks

Diet A wide variety of invertebrates as well as smaller vertebrates and carrion; also feeds on vegetable matter and fruit

Habitat Most likely to be encountered in open areas of woodland; sometimes also occurs in marshy areas

Distribution Eastern United States to northern Mexico

Status Has declined in various parts of its range

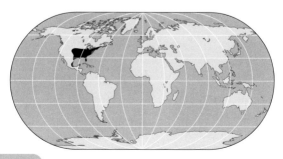

Spotted Turtle

Common name Spotted turtle

Scientific name *Clemmys guttata*

Family Emydidae

Suborder Cryptodira

Order Testudines

Size Carapace to a maximum length of 5 in (13 cm)

Weight Approximately 1.1 lb (0.5 kg)

Key features Carapace relatively low and blackish with an overlying pattern of yellowish spots (which may be more orange in some cases); plastron varies from yellowish to orange in color with variable black blotching; males have brownish chin and eyes; females are more colorful with orange irises and a yellow chin as well as a flatter plastron

Habits Semiaquatic, often wandering on land as well as being found in water

Breeding Female lays a single clutch of 3–8 eggs that hatch after about 10 weeks

Diet Omnivorous; eats especially invertebrates of various types, some of which may be captured on land

Habitat Typically found in marshy areas, sometimes in association with woodland

Distribution North America from the Great Lakes in southern Canada south to northern Florida

Status May be under threat in some areas from habitat disturbance and loss

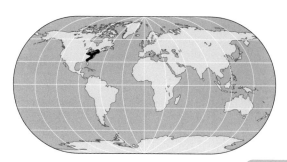

Asian Leaf Turtle

Common name Asian leaf turtle (leaf turtle)

Scientific name *Cyclemys dentata*

Family Emydidae

Suborder Cryptodira

Order Testudines

Size Carapace up to 9.5 in (24 cm) long ; females tend to be larger overall than males

Weight Up to 2.2 lb (1 kg)

Key features Carapace flattened and rounded, light brown through olive to black in color with a keel running down the midline; plastron is light yellowish and narrow compared with carapace; head reddish brown on top and a darker shade of brown on the sides; toes moderately webbed; adults have a hinged plastron

Habits Semiaquatic; moves quite well on land; may climb trees

Breeding Female lays small clutches of 2–3 eggs several times during the year; eggs hatch after about 2–3 months

Diet Omnivorous, eating both plant and animal matter

Habitat Usually found in or near shallow streams

Distribution Found throughout much of Southeast Asia, including Indonesian and Philippine islands

Status Not uncommon in some areas, but the population has probably declined overall; Lower Risk (IUCN)

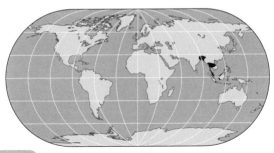

Galápagos Giant Tortoise

Common name Galápagos giant tortoise

Scientific name *Geochelone nigra*

Family Testudinidae

Suborder Cryptodira

Order Testudines

Size Carapace from 29 in (74 cm) to over 4 ft (1.2 m) long depending on subspecies

Weight Approximately 500 lb (227 kg)

Key features Large, bulky tortoise; shell shape varies depending on subspecies; neck often long; carapace and plastron are a uniform dull shade of brown; males have longer, thicker tails than females and often have a more yellowish area on the lower jaw and throat

Habits Seeks out sun in the morning, basking before setting off to feed; usually inactive in the latter part of the afternoon, sometimes wallowing in a muddy hollow; quite agile despite its large size

Breeding Female lays clutch of 2-10 eggs, occasionally up to 16; eggs hatch usually after 3-4 months

Diet A wide range of vegetation and fruit; can even eat the spiny shoots of the prickly pear cactus

Habitat Generally prefers upland areas

Distribution Restricted to the Galápagos Islands

Status Endangered, critically in some cases (IUCN)

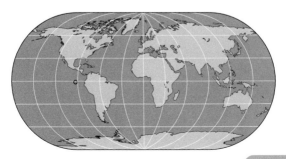

Gopher Tortoises

Gopher tortoise
(*Gopherus
polyphemus*)

Common/scientific names Desert gopher, *Gopherus agassizii*; gopher tortoise, *G. polyphemus*; Berlandier's gopher, *G. berlandieri*; Bolson tortoise, *G. flavomarginatus*

Family Testudinidae

Suborder Cryptodira

Order Testudines

Size Carapace length from 9 in (23 cm) in *G. berlandieri* to 20 in (50 cm) in *G. agassizii*

Weight Approximately 8 lb (3.6 kg) to 15 lb (6.8 kg)

Key features Carapace domed; front limbs flattened for burrowing and bear thick hard scales; hind feet stumpy and elephantine; all feet lack webbing; plastron in males is concave; carapace generally some shade of brown or tan but variable according to species; plastron usually yellowish

Habits Strictly terrestrial; retreat into burrows to avoid excessive temperatures; desert gophers and Bolson tortoises may hibernate

Breeding Most mate in spring, and females may nest 2 or 3 times a season; all are egg layers, with clutch sizes ranging from 2–15 eggs that hatch in late summer or fall

Diet Herbivores; diet includes plants, fruits, and grasses

Habitat Preference for sandy soil; varies from arid desert to scrub woodlands, grasslands, and forests

Distribution Southern United States south to Mexico

Status Numbers in decline due to habitat change and land development; *G. polypheumus*, *G. flavomarginatus*, and *G. agassizii* are Vulnerable (IUCN); all species listed on CITES Appendix I or II

Leopard Tortoise

Common name Leopard tortoise

Scientific name *Geochelone pardalis*

Family Testudinidae

Suborder Cryptodira

Order Testudines

Size Carapace to a maximum of 24 in (60 cm) long

Weight Up to 70 lb (32 kg)

Key features Carapace domed and attractive with a variable pattern of dark markings on a light yellowish-horn background; skin is relatively light in color, but some individuals are darker overall than others; male has a longer tail than female, and its plastron is slightly concave; young hatchlings have egg tooth on snout

Habits Wanders through grassland and savanna; diurnal

Breeding Female lays individual clutches ranging from 5–30 eggs; eggs hatch after 8–18 months

Diet Eats virtually all plant matter, including dry grass when other food is in short supply

Habitat Open areas of country

Distribution Eastern and southern parts of Africa from Ethiopia south to the Cape

Status Relatively common but at risk from being hunted for food

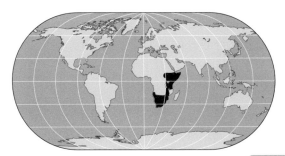

Red-Headed Rock Agama

Common name Red-headed rock agama (rainbow lizard)

Scientific name *Agama agama*

Family Agamidae

Suborder Sauria

Order Squamata

Size 12 in (30 cm) long; males larger than females

Key features Body stocky; limbs and tail long; head wide and triangular; dominant males strikingly colored with blue body and yellow, orange, or brick-red head and a white stripe down the center of their back; subordinate males are duller; females and juveniles brown with spots of white and black

Habits Diurnal; terrestrial but climbs vertical surfaces well

Breeding Females lay 5–10 eggs in loose soil; eggs hatch after 50–60 days

Diet Insects, including ants; some plant material

Habitat Rocky places in deserts, grasslands, and sparse woodlands; often seen on and around buildings

Distribution West, central, and East Africa

Status Very common

Similar species There are many other agamas; females are easily confused with each other; males are distinctive, but the Mwanza flat-headed agama, *A. mwanzae*, is similar; however, its head is pink rather than orange-red

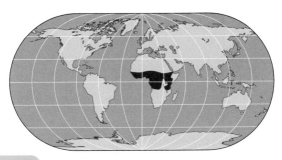

Common Flying Lizard

Common name
Common flying
lizard (flying dragon)

Scientific name *Draco volans*

Family Agamidae

Suborder Sauria

Order Squamata

Size From 6 in (15 cm) to 8 in (20 cm) long

Key features Body slender with a long, thin tail and long, spindly legs; there is a flap of skin on each side of the body supported by elongated ribs; these "wings" are normally held against the side of the body but can be opened for gliding; wings are mottled orange and black; both sexes have a dewlap (piece of loose skin) on their throat that is yellow in males and blue in females

Habits Diurnal; arboreal, living on vertical tree trunks

Breeding Egg layer with clutches of 3–6 eggs buried in the ground

Diet Small insects, mainly ants and termites

Habitat Rain forests

Distribution Southeast Asia (Malaysian Peninsula, Indonesia, Borneo, and the Philippines)

Status Common

Similar species There are 28 species of flying lizard altogether, and their ranges overlap in many places; they are most easily distinguished by the color of their wings and dewlaps

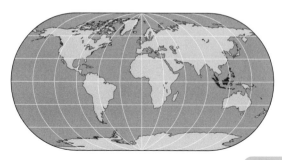

Frilled Lizard

Common name Frilled lizard

Scientific name *Chlamydosaurus kingii*

Family Agamidae

Suborder Sauria

Order Squamata

Size From 24 in (61 cm) to 36 in (91 cm) long

Key features A large lizard with a triangular head and a wide, circular frill around its neck; frill is normally folded along its neck and chest when at rest but raised when the lizard is alarmed; body usually brown; frill can range from brown to black, the latter having a red center

Habits Arboreal; diurnal

Breeding Egg layer with 8–14 eggs per clutch; eggs hatch after 54–92 days

Diet Insects and small vertebrates, including other lizards

Habitat Open woodland

Distribution North Australia and southern New Guinea

Status Common

Similar species None

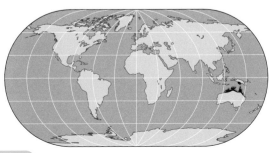

Thorny Devil

Common name Thorny devil

Scientific name *Moloch horridus*

Family Agamidae

Suborder Sauria

Order Squamata

Size From 6 in (15 cm) to 7 in (18 cm) long

Key features A weird-looking lizard; body squat, covered in large, thornlike spines; there is a very large spine over each eye, a raised, spiny hump on its neck, and 2 rows of spines along the top of its tail; dark reddish brown in color with wavy-edged, light tan stripes running over its head and down its body

Habits Diurnal; terrestrial; slow moving

Breeding Egg layer with a single clutch of 3–10 eggs; eggs hatch after 90–132 days

Diet Ants

Habitat Deserts

Distribution Western and central Australia

Status Probably common in suitable habitat but rarely seen

Similar species There is nothing remotely similar in the region

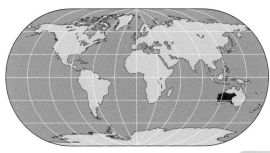

Central Bearded Dragon

Common name Central bearded dragon

Scientific name *Pogona vitticeps*

Family Agamidae

Suborder Sauria

Order Squamata

Size From 12 in (30 cm) to 16 in (41 cm) long

Key features A thickset lizard with a slightly flattened body; back and neck covered with large spiny scales interspersed with smaller ones; a row of large conical scales runs around the edges of the back where it meets the underside; usually light brown in color but can also be yellowish brown or reddish brown; it has faint crossbands down the back and tail and stripes on its head that fade with age; throat is darker than the body, sometimes black

Habits Diurnal; terrestrial

Breeding Egg layer with large clutches of up to 35 eggs; eggs hatch after about 60 days

Diet Insects and plant material, especially flowers

Habitat Arid deserts and dry woodlands

Distribution Central Australia

Status Common

Similar species The eastern bearded dragon, *P. barbata*, lacks the row of conical scales along its flanks

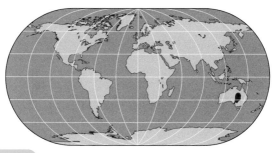

African Dwarf Chameleons

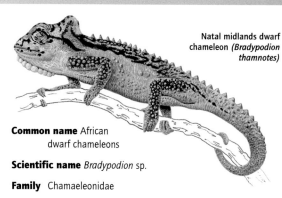

Natal midlands dwarf chameleon (*Bradypodion thamnotes*)

Common name African dwarf chameleons

Scientific name *Bradypodion* sp.

Family Chamaeleonidae

Suborder Sauria

Order Squamata

Number of species 21

Size From 4.5 in (11 cm) to 8 in (20 cm) long

Key features Crests of small tubercles present along the back and throat; larger tubercles on body, legs, and tail; small to medium casque; faint dorsal and gular crests; females, juveniles, and males are usually mottled greens and browns in color outside the breeding season; displaying males can be spectacular; *Bradypodion* sp. differ from other chameleons in that they have single-lobed lungs

Habits Arboreal, climbing to the top of vegetation to bask; nights spent in denser vegetation for safety and warmth

Breeding Live-bearers; females produce 3 litters a year with about 12–15 babies in each litter; gestation lasts 3–5 months depending on species; species living at higher altitudes have the longer gestation period

Diet A wide variety of crawling and flying insects

Habitat From montane forest to coastal fynbos that offer grass, heathers, and low bushes; some species inhabit parks and gardens

Distribution South Africa

Status Setaro's dwarf chameleon, *B. setaroi*—Endangered (IUCN); Smith's dwarf chameleon, *B. taeniabronchum*—Critical (IUCN); others common locally

Similar species None

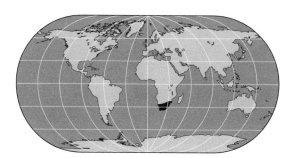

Stump-Tailed Chameleon

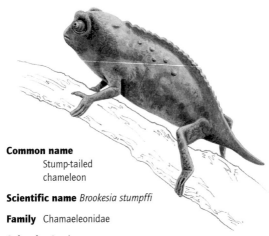

Common name
Stump-tailed chameleon

Scientific name *Brookesia stumpffi*

Family Chamaeleonidae

Suborder Sauria

Order Squamata

Size 3.5 in (9 cm) long

Key features Skull triangular shaped; tail relatively short compared with other genera and only faintly prehensile; curved crest over eye; body elongated; dorsal crest made up of paired spiny scales; legs and casque have pointed sharp scales; there is a plate over the base of the tail that extends onto each side; color brownish gray or green

Habits Diurnal, spending most of the time hunting insects in leaf litter; becomes more active during the rainy season

Breeding Females lay up to 2 clutches a year, usually in January or February; each clutch contains 2 or sometimes 4 eggs; eggs hatch after 6–8 weeks

Diet Insects such as small flies, termites, small beetles, and young mantids

Habitat Leaf litter and vegetation up to 39 in (100 cm) from the ground

Distribution North and northwestern Madagascar, including the island of Nosy Bé

Status Common

Similar species *Brookesia ebenaui* and *B. superciliaris*

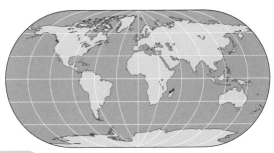

Parson's Chameleon

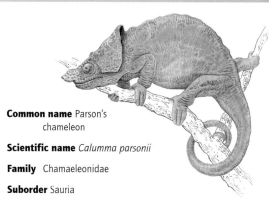

Common name Parson's chameleon

Scientific name *Calumma parsonii*

Family Chamaeleonidae

Suborder Sauria

Order Squamata

Size Usually up to 24 in (60 cm) long

Key features Males have paired, warty rostral processes; both sexes have occipital lobes (flaps) at the back of the head; no dorsal or ventral crest; male coloration is turquoise-blue with yellow or orange eyes; females are a uniform green; the casque and forehead are brown; 4 or 5 darker diagonal lines break up the coloration on the flanks; both sexes have a pale yellow or white spot in the center of the flanks

Habits Slow moving, inactive for most of the day; remains in one place if temperatures are within its requirements, and water and food are available; does not like to bask for extended periods; prefers filtered sunlight

Breeding Females lay 1 clutch of 40–60 eggs per year; eggs take about 21–23 months to hatch

Diet Large insects such as grasshoppers, butterflies, moths, stick and leaf insects, cockroaches; also small mammals and birds

Habitat Rain forests; prefers primary (untouched) forest with cool, humid conditions; rarely adapts to secondary forest

Distribution There are isolated populations on the eastern coast of Madagascar; also northern Madagascar and the islands of Nosy Boraha and Nosy Bé (yellow-lipped form)

Status Common locally

Similar species *Calumma globifer* and *C. oshaughnessyi*

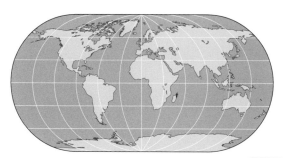

Veiled Chameleon

Common name Veiled chameleon (Yemen chameleon)

Scientific name *Chamaeleo calyptratus*

Family Chamaeleonidae

Suborder Sauria

Order Squamata

Size From 16 in (41 cm) to 20 in (50 cm) long

Key features High, laterally compressed casque; scales of different sizes; coloration of males consists of light yellow bands alternating with bluish-green bands; gular area and underside paler bluish green; females light green; both sexes have a row of white patches on both sides

Habits Sun loving and more heat tolerant than most other species of chameleons

Breeding Female lays up to 3 clutches a year, each containing 12–20 eggs; eggs hatch after 6–8 months

Diet Large insects (grasshoppers, locusts, spiders), small lizards and geckos, small mammals, and plant matter

Habitat Mountainous regions, dry forested areas in valleys, and riverbeds with oases; areas range from lush, semitropical vegetation to arid deserts

Distribution San'a and Dhamer in western Yemen; the subspecies *C. c. calcarifer* occurs along the southwestern coast of Saudi Arabia

Status Common

Similar species None

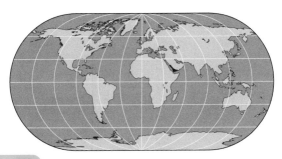

Jackson's Chameleon

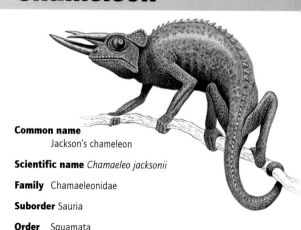

Common name
Jackson's chameleon

Scientific name *Chamaeleo jacksonii*

Family Chamaeleonidae

Suborder Sauria

Order Squamata

Size 12 in (30 cm) long

Key features 3 horns present on the head—2 at eye level (orbital), the 3rd located on the tip of the snout (rostral) and curving upward; dorsal crest of prominent tubercles gives the impression of a saw blade; female's horns much reduced or absent; basic coloration green; small crest to the rear of the head is outlined by conical scales

Habits Solitary, each with its own territory; individuals from middle elevations hold their body perpendicular to sun's rays to warm up in the morning; color changes to yellow when it becomes too warm; moves into deep foliage for shade and to begin feeding

Breeding Live-bearer; female produces 1 or 2 clutches a year; each clutch contains up to 35 young; gestation period about 6–9 months

Diet Insects, particularly grasshoppers, butterflies, katydids, spiders, and flies

Habitat High altitudes; found at elevations of 8,000 ft (2,440 m) that have high rainfall and distinct wet and dry seasons leading to fluctuations in temperature and humidity; common in primary and secondary forest

Distribution Mountains of Kenya and Tanzania (East Africa); introduced to Hawaii

Status Common

Similar species *Chamaeleo johnstonii* (although this species is an egg layer)

Panther Chameleon

Common name
Panther chameleon

Scientific name *Furcifer pardalis*

Family Chamaeleonidae

Suborder Sauria

Order Squamata

Size From 15 in (38 cm) to 22 in (56 cm) long depending on locality; female a little smaller

Key features Males and females differ in color, shape, and size; male has a prominent rostral ridge (less prominent in female); snout bears enlarged scales; males vary from blue to green to pink depending on location; females grayish fawn or light pinkish brown; both sexes have a lateral line of whitish or bluish oval blotches

Habits Lives on small shrubs or even weeds in deforested areas; on cool days it basks, on warm days it sits in partial shade

Breeding Female lays 2–4 clutches a year; clutch size 12–45 eggs; eggs hatch after 6–13 months

Diet Large insects, small mammals, small lizards and geckos; in some localities small frogs are eaten

Habitat Forest edge; agricultural and suburban areas

Distribution Eastern coast and coastal islands of northern and eastern Madagascar; small populations on Reunion Island and Mauritius

Status Common

Similar species None

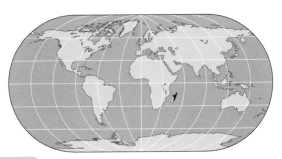

Western Pygmy Chameleon

Common name Western pygmy chameleon
(leaf chameleon, African pygmy chameleon)

Scientific name *Rhampholeon spectrum*

Family Chamaeleonidae

Suborder Sauria

Order Squamata

Size 3 in (8 cm) long

Key features Small rostral appendage (often mistaken for a
horn); slightly raised casque to rear of head; dorsal crest
made up of regular-shaped tubercles; tail relatively short
and only faintly prehensile; lateral ridge along sides of
body; tiny spines on underside of feet; body color brown
with 2 diagonal black stripes

Habits Spends most of the day on forest floor in leaf litter,
foraging for insects; at night perches on branches
36 in (91 cm) above the floor

Breeding Female lays up to 4 clutches of 2–4 eggs per year;
eggs hatch after 6–8 weeks

Diet Spiders, crickets, small cockroaches, termites

Habitat Evergreen and semievergreen rain forest near sea level
and montane cloud forest up to 6,250 ft (1,900 m)

Distribution West Africa (Congo, Gabon, Equatorial Guinea, and
Cameroon)

Status Common

Similar species *Rhampholeon affinis* and *R. boulengeri*

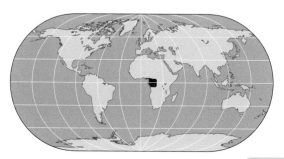

Plumed Basilisk

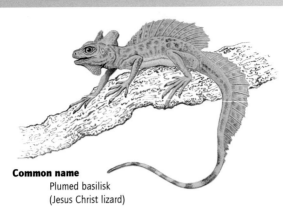

Common name
Plumed basilisk
(Jesus Christ lizard)

Scientific name *Basiliscus plumifrons*

Subfamily Corytophaninae

Family Iguanidae

Suborder Sauria

Order Squamata

Size Males to 36 inches (91 cm) long; females to 20 inches (51 cm), of which the tail can account for three-quarters

Key features Adults green with black bars on the tail and lighter green or white spots on the flanks; both sexes have a crest on their head (the male's has 2 lobes); male also has separate crests on the back and tail; body and tail flattened from side to side; front legs and tail very long; juveniles are spidery in appearance with long, thin legs

Habits Arboreal or semiarboreal; diurnal

Breeding Egg layer that breeds throughout the year; female lays 4-17 eggs that hatch after about 65 days

Diet Small vertebrates, invertebrates, and plant material

Habitat Forests (usually in the vicinity of water)

Distribution Central America (eastern Honduras to southwestern Costa Rica)

Status Common in suitable habitat

Similar species There are other basilisks in the region, but *B. plumifrons* is the only bright green one; other green iguanids of similar size lack crests

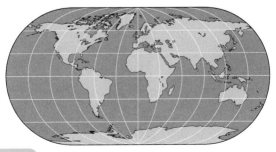

Collared Lizard

Common name Collared lizard

Scientific name *Crotaphytus collaris*

Subfamily Crotaphytinae

Family Iguanidae

Suborder Sauria

Order Squamata

Size To 10 in (25cm) long; males are larger than females

Key features Head massive; 2 black rings around the neck; tail long and cylindrical; hind limbs long; body covered in small scales, giving the skin a silky texture; body color varies among populations and with the season but is typically green in males, dull green, brown, or yellowish in females, all with light spots loosely arranged into transverse lines; juveniles have distinct banding across the back that gradually fades as the animal grows

Habits Diurnal and heat loving; lives on the ground and rarely climbs, except among boulders

Breeding Egg layer with more than 1 clutch each year; female lays 1–13 eggs that hatch after about 45 days

Diet Large invertebrates and smaller lizards; also some vegetable material, including leaves and flowers

Habitat Hot, rocky hillsides with sparse vegetation

Distribution Western United States in desert regions

Status Common

Similar species There are other collared lizards, but their ranges do not overlap; the leopard lizards, *Gambelia*, are their only other close relatives

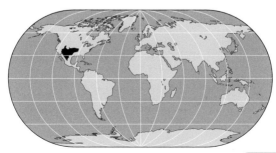

Marine Iguana

Common name Marine iguana

Scientific name *Amblyrhynchus cristatus*

Subfamily Iguaninae

Family Iguanidae

Suborder Sauria

Order Squamata

Size From 30 in (75 cm) to 4.1 ft (1.3 m)

Key features Heavy bodied with muscular limbs and a powerful
tail; a crest of elongated, toothlike scales runs along the
center of the back and tail; top of the head covered with
horny, conical scales of varying sizes; color usually gray,
although some subspecies are more colorful with
patches of red or turquoise

Habits Diurnal, basking by day on rocks and entering the
sea to feed

Breeding Egg layer; female lays 1–6 eggs in tunnels on shore;
eggs hatch after about 95 days

Diet Marine algae (seaweed)

Habitat Rocky seashores

Distribution Galápagos Islands

Status Protected under national legislation but possibly at risk
in the long term from human pressures

Similar species The marine iguana is unmistakable; the only
other iguanas on the islands are the Galápagos land
iguanas, *Conolophus subcristatus*, and the much smaller
lava lizards, *Microlophus* sp.

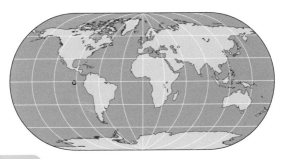

Galápagos Land Iguana

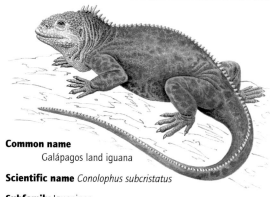

Common name
Galápagos land iguana

Scientific name *Conolophus subcristatus*

Subfamily Iguaninae

Family Iguanidae

Suborder Sauria

Order Squamata

Size To 39 in (100 cm) long

Key features Heavy bodied and ponderous with pointed scales covering the head; a low crest of small, tooth-shaped scales runs along the ridge of the back and onto the tail; limbs short, thick, and powerful; toes end in long claws used for digging burrows; color variable with head, limbs, and flanks ranging from uniform dark brown to a pattern of bright golden yellow; back darker

Habits Diurnal; terrestrial but sometimes climbs into shrubs in search of food

Breeding Egg layer; female lays up to 25 eggs

Diet Vegetation, especially the pads and fruits of prickly pear cacti, *Opuntia* sp.

Habitat Hot, dry, rocky islands

Distribution Galápagos Islands; at present only found on Santa Cruz, Isabela, Fernandina, Plaza Sur, North Seymour, and Baltra

Status Secure on some islands, dwindling on others; extinct from many islands where it once lived

Similar species The pale land iguana, *C. pallidus*, is similar but light grayish brown in color and restricted to a single island, Santa Fé

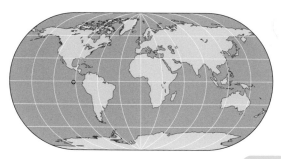

115

Green Iguana

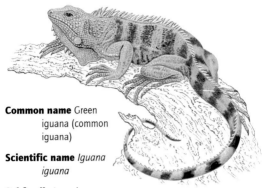

Common name Green iguana (common iguana)

Scientific name *Iguana iguana*

Subfamily Iguaninae

Family Iguanidae

Suborder Sauria

Order Squamata

Size Males to 6.6 ft (2 m) long, females to 4.8 ft (1.4 m)

Key features Very large green or greenish lizards; adults have crest of tooth-shaped scales along the back and the first third of the tail; tail has broad, dark bands around it; limbs long; each toe is also long and has claws for grasping; large males develop a flap of skin (dewlap) under the chin (in females it is smaller); a single, very large smooth scale present on each side of the head below the eardrum in both males and females

Habits Arboreal; diurnal

Breeding Egg layers with large clutches of 9–71 eggs; eggs hatch after 65–115 days

Diet Mostly vegetation, especially leaves

Habitat Forests, especially rain forests but also dry deciduous forests in some places

Distribution Central and South America (northwestern Mexico in the north to Ecuador, northern Bolivia, Paraguay, and southern Brazil to the south); also on some West Indian islands and introduced to Florida

Status Common in places but under pressure from humans in others

Similar species The closely related *I. delicatissima* from the Lesser Antilles (West Indies)

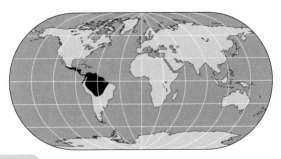

Coast Horned Lizard

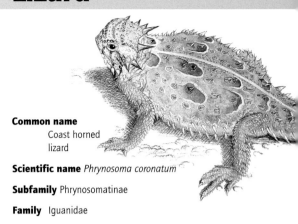

Common name
Coast horned
lizard

Scientific name *Phrynosoma coronatum*

Subfamily Phrynosomatinae

Family Iguanidae

Suborder Sauria

Order Squamata

Size From 2.5 in (6 cm) to 4 in (10 cm)

Key features Body flattened and oval or disk shaped; head has a crest, or "coronet," of long, backward-pointing spines, the central 2 (the "horns") being longer than the others; a fringe of smaller thorny spines runs along the edge on each side of its body; large spiny scales also scattered over its back; color yellow, beige, or pale pink with irregular darker crossbands and a paler stripe down the center, providing camouflage colors to match the sand or gravel on which it is resting

Habits Diurnal; terrestrial

Breeding Egg layer with an average of 25 eggs laid in the summer; eggs hatch after about 60 days

Diet Small invertebrates, especially ants

Habitat Dry scrub and sandy washes with scattered bushes; also in dry forest clearings

Distribution Western California south to the tip of Baja California, Mexico

Status Common but easily overlooked

Similar species There are other horned lizards in the American Southwest, but none of their ranges overlap that of this species; the 2 long spines on the back of its head are also distinctive

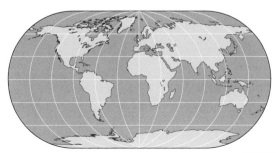

Green Anole

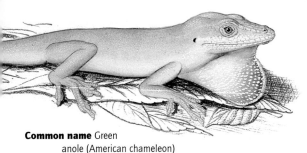

Common name Green anole (American chameleon)

Scientific name *Anolis carolinensis*

Subfamily Polychrotinae

Family Iguanidae

Suborder Sauria

Order Squamata

Size From 4.5 in (11 cm) to 8 in (20 cm) long

Key features A graceful lizard; head long and narrow; snout pointed; body long and slender; tail nearly twice as long as head and body combined; legs long and thin; toes have small pads just behind the claws for climbing; color usually bright green but can change to brown or buff; males have a pink dewlap (throat flap)

Habits Diurnal; arboreal, climbing mainly in shrubs and on tree trunks

Breeding Egg layer; female lays several clutches containing a single egg throughout the summer

Diet Small invertebrates

Habitat Open woodland, hedges, parks, and gardens

Distribution Southeastern North America

Status Formerly common, now becoming increasingly rare

Similar species None in the area; small introduced anoles in Florida lack the bright green coloration; the knight anole, *A. equestris*, is much larger and lives only in the extreme south of Florida

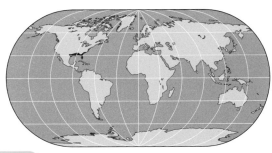

Side-Blotched Lizard

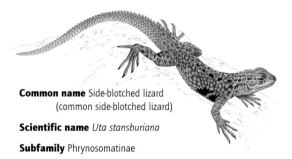

Common name Side-blotched lizard (common side-blotched lizard)

Scientific name *Uta stansburiana*

Subfamily Phrynosomatinae

Family Iguanidae

Suborder Sauria

Order Squamata

Size From 3 in (7.5 cm) to 5 in (13 cm) long

Key features Body small, brownish or gray; small rounded scales give it a smooth appearance; no dorsal crest; a dark black or bluish blotch usually present on either side of the body just behind the front limbs; males may have blue flecks and orange or yellow on their throat and sides

Habits Diurnal; terrestrial, may climb into low shrubs

Breeding Egg layer; female lays several clutches during the summer; eggs hatch after about 60 days

Diet Insects and other invertebrates

Habitat Anywhere dry; sand dunes and washes, scrub, places with scattered rocks and thin woodlands

Distribution Southwestern United States from Washington to western Texas south to Baja California, Sonora, and north-central Mexico

Status Very common

Similar species The tree lizard, *Urosaurus microscutatus*, has a double row of large scales along its midline interrupted by a single row of small ones down the center; the long-tailed brush lizard, *Urosaurus graciosus*, has a wide band of large scales down its back; both lack the characteristic dark blotch of *Uta stansburiana*

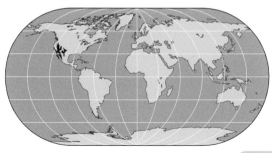

Leopard Gecko

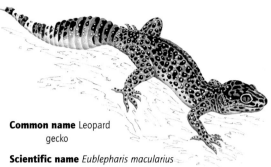

Common name Leopard gecko

Scientific name *Eublepharis macularius*

Subfamily Eublepharinae

Family Eublepharidae

Suborder Sauria

Order Squamata

Size 8 in (20 cm) to 10 in (25 cm) long

Key features This species has eyelids; head broad; body cylindrical; tail is thick and carrot shaped when animal is well fed; skin covered with small tubercles; toes lack adhesive pads; color yellow or tan with many small, dark-brown spots over the top of the head, back, and tail, sometimes with bluish background; spots on tail superimposed on wide black-and-white bands; juveniles are completely different with wide, saddle-shaped, dark-brown markings on a white or cream background

Habits Terrestrial and nocturnal; seeks refuge from the heat by day and from the cold in winter by living in underground burrows

Breeding Female lays 2 soft-shelled eggs; eggs hatch after 40–60 days

Diet Invertebrates, including insects, spiders, and scorpions; also other lizards

Habitat Desert and scrub regions in mountainous areas

Distribution South-central Asia (Pakistan, northwest India, Iraq, Iran, and Afghanistan)

Status Common

Similar species Other poorly known species of *Eublepharis* occur in the region and are similar to the leopard gecko

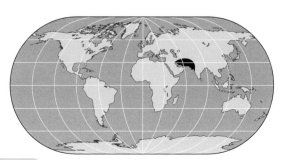

Western Banded Gecko

Common name Western banded gecko

Scientific name *Coleonyx variegatus*

Subfamily Eublepharinae

Family Eublepharidae

Suborder Sauria

Order Squamata

Size From 3.3 in (8 cm) to 4.3 in (12 cm) long

Key features A delicate-looking gecko with thin, translucent skin and tiny scales; eyes are large and have functional eyelids; limbs long and thin; toes end in small claws; color variable but usually cream, buff, or yellow with dark-brown crossbands; tail has black-and-white bands

Habits Terrestrial; strictly nocturnal

Breeding Female lays 2 soft-shelled eggs; eggs hatch after about 45 days

Diet Insects, spiders, and small scorpions

Habitat Rocky deserts

Distribution Southwestern United Sates and northwestern Mexico, including Baja California

Status Common

Similar species There are 6 other members of the genus, but a combination of range, size, and markings makes it unlikely that they would be confused with the western banded gecko (or each other)

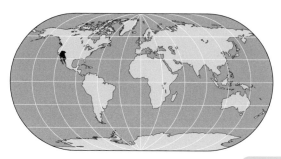

Giant Leaf-Tailed Gecko

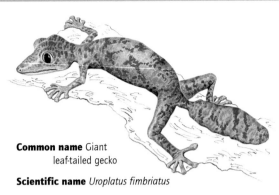

Common name Giant leaf-tailed gecko

Scientific name *Uroplatus fimbriatus*

Subfamily Gekkoninae

Family Gekkonidae

Suborder Sauria

Order Squamata

Size Up to 12 in (30 cm) long and therefore one of the largest geckos in the world

Key features Body large and flattened; head large and triangular; eyes cream in color, massive and bulging with intricate markings; tail flattened and leaflike; toes have expanded pads for climbing and clinging; a frill of skin present around the lower jaw and along the flanks; coloration plain or mottled gray or brown, but it can change from light to dark possibly in response to temperature

Habits Strictly arboreal and nocturnal

Breeding Female lays 2 hard-shelled eggs; eggs hatch after about 77–84 days

Diet Invertebrates and possibly smaller lizards

Habitat Rain forests

Distribution Eastern Madagascar

Status Common in suitable habitat but hard to find

Similar species *Uroplatus henkeli* is very similar but has a more strongly patterned back, is slightly smaller, and has a different eye color; other species of *Uroplatus* are significantly smaller and are more easily distinguished from this species

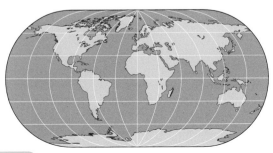

Tokay Gecko

Common name Tokay gecko

Scientific name *Gekko gecko*

Subfamily Gekkoninae

Family Gekkonidae

Suborder Sauria

Order Squamata

Size From 8 in (20 cm) to 14 in (36 cm) long

Key features A large, heavy-bodied gecko with a massive head, prominent yellow or orange eyes, and a huge gape; conspicuous toe pads present; skin covered in small granular scales interspersed with raised tubercles; color bluish gray with evenly scattered spots of lighter blue and rust

Habits Naturally arboreal but also found on the walls of buildings; nocturnal

Breeding Female lays 2 (sometimes 3) spherical, hard-shelled eggs; eggs usually hatch after about 100 days

Diet Invertebrates of all sizes and small vertebrates, including other geckos

Habitat Forests, plantations, and buildings

Distribution Southeast Asia

Status Very common

Similar species The green-eyed gecko, *G. smithii*, is about the same size but gray in color with emerald-green eyes

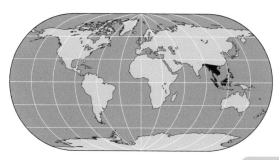

Ashy Gecko

Common name Ashy gecko

Scientific name *Sphaerodactylus elegans*

Subfamily Sphaerodactylinae

Family Gekkonidae

Suborder Sauria

Order Squamata

Size 2.8 in (7.1 cm) long

Key features Head pointed and flattened; body and tail cylindrical with a speckled pattern of yellowish-brown markings on a darker background; markings sometimes run together to form stripes or parts of stripes, especially on the head; toe pads present on digits, but they are small and easily overlooked; juveniles are gray with dark crossbands and a reddish tail

Habits Diurnal and terrestrial or arboreal

Breeding Female lays a single hard-shelled egg; further details unkown

Diet Small insects and spiders

Habitat Rarely seen away from buildings but thought to live naturally in forests and plantations

Distribution Cuba, Hispaniola; introduced to Florida

Status Common

Similar species All *Sphaerodactylus* species look similar; in Florida *S. elegans* is the only small gecko with many small pale spots covering the entire head, body, and tail; separation from other West Indian species can be very difficult

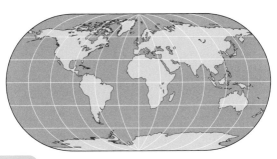

Moorish Gecko

Common name Moorish gecko
(common wall gecko, crocodile gecko)

Scientific name *Tarentola mauretanica*

Subfamily Gekkoninae

Family Gekkonidae

Suborder Sauria

Order Squamata

Size 6 in (15 cm) long

Key features Heavily built; head wide; mouth large; large, slightly spiky scales on its back, sides, and tail give it a roughened appearance; color light or dark gray with darker bands across the body and tail, most obvious in juveniles; small red marks often present between its toes caused by parasitic gecko mites

Habits Nocturnal, living on walls and rock faces; it will also live among rocks on the ground; occasionally basks during the day

Breeding Female lays up to 15 clutches of 1 or (more commonly) 2 hard-shelled eggs; eggs hatch after 44–75 days

Diet Invertebrates

Habitat Dry places, including stone and plaster walls, tiles, cliffs, and woodpiles

Distribution Mediterranean (Spain, Portugal, coastal regions of France, Italy, Greece, and North Africa; also many large and small islands)

Status Very common

Similar species Other *Tarentola* species, from which it is best distinguished by distribution; the other Mediterranean gecko is the Turkish gecko, *Hemidactylus turcicus*, which is smaller and has a pale-pinkish, translucent skin

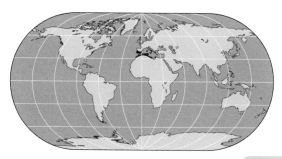

Web-Footed Gecko

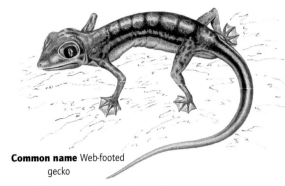

Common name Web-footed gecko

Scientific name *Palmatogecko rangei*

Subfamily Gekkoninae

Family Gekkonidae

Suborder Sauria

Order Squamata

Size From 4 in (10 cm) to 5 in (13 cm) long

Key features A delicate gecko with small scales and translucent, smooth skin; characterized by webbing between the toes and prominent, large, colorful eyes situated on top of the head; color pinkish above with faint netting of a darker shade and white below; the 2 colors meet abruptly along the flanks; limbs thin and spindly

Habits Terrestrial and nocturnal; escapes the daytime heat by resting in a burrow

Breeding Female lays several clutches each containing 2 hard-shelled eggs; eggs hatch after 55–90 days

Diet Small invertebrates, especially termites, crickets, grasshoppers, and beetles

Habitat Sand dunes

Distribution Namib Desert from the Richtersveld of South Africa to extreme southern Angola

Status Common in suitable habitat

Similar species The Kaoko web-footed gecko, *P. vanzyli*, also lives in the Namib Desert but is restricted to gravel plains in the north; it is similar to the web-footed gecko, but only its hind feet are webbed

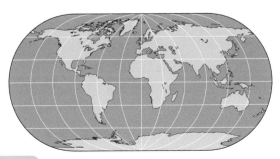

Day Geckos

Gold-dust day gecko
(Phelsuma laticauda)

Common name Day geckos

Scientific name *Phelsuma* sp.

Subfamily Gekkoninae

Family Gekkonidae

Suborder Sauria

Order Squamata

Number of species 40

Size From 4 in (10 cm) to 12 in (30 cm) long

Key features Expanded toe pads present; eyes smaller than in other geckos; pupils circular; scales on the back small and granular; color mostly bright green often with red markings; a few of the larger species are dull olive or grayish green; both sexes usually the same color

Habits Arboreal and diurnal

Breeding Females lay 2 hard-shelled eggs and either stick them to a vertical surface, hide them in a hollow stem, or bury them in the ground; eggs hatch after 35–60 days

Diet Insects, fruit, and nectar

Habitat Forests, plantations, and clearings, often on the trunks of palms and other large trees; some species found around human habitats, others restricted to undisturbed forests

Distribution Southwest Africa (1 species), East Africa, Madagascar, the Comoros Islands, Mascarene Islands, and other Indian Ocean island groups as far east as the Andaman Islands

Status Mostly fairly common, but some species live in very restricted habitats

Similar species Effectively none; a few other brightly colored geckos either do not occur in the same region or are not bright green

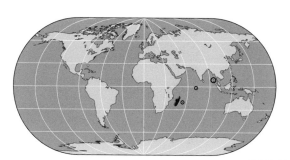

Barking Gecko

Common name Barking gecko

Scientific name *Ptenopus garrulus*

Subfamily Gekkoninae

Family Gekkonidae

Suborder Sauria

Order Squamata

Size 4 in (10 cm) long

Key features Chunky gecko with a rounded head, blunt snout, and large, bulging eyes; face appears to have a permanent "grin"; toes lack adhesive pads but have a fringe of pointed scales along the edges; back, head, and tail are brown, gray, or reddish brown with intricate marblings of light and dark spots; underside is white; male has a yellow throat

Habits Nocturnal and terrestrial

Breeding Female lays 2 hard-shelled eggs; further details unknown

Diet Small invertebrates such as termites, ants, and small beetles

Habitat Desert flats with hard-packed sand or gravelly surfaces

Distribution Southern Africa (central and northwestern South Africa, most of Namibia and Central Botswana as far as extreme southern Zimbabwe)

Status Common in suitable habitat

Similar species 2 other barking geckos from the same region, Carp's barking gecko, *P. carpi*, and Koch's barking gecko, *P. kochi*, have restricted ranges in the Namib Desert

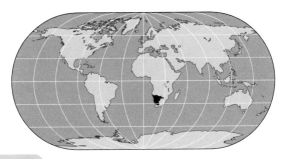

Kuhl's Flying Gecko

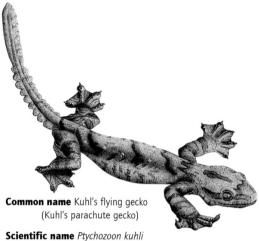

Common name Kuhl's flying gecko (Kuhl's parachute gecko)

Scientific name *Ptychozoon kuhli*

Subfamily Gekkoninae

Family Gekkonidae

Suborder Sauria

Order Squamata

Size 8 in (20 cm) long

Key features A frilly gecko; a flap of skin is present along the flanks between the front and hind limbs, and there is a scalloped frill on the edges of the tail; feet are webbed, and toes have adhesive pads; head, body, and tail are brown, gray, or olive in color with broken bands and patches of darker coloration, making the gecko well camouflaged

Habits Arboreal and nocturnal

Breeding Female lays 2 hard-shelled eggs; eggs hatch after about 100 days

Diet Insects and spiders

Habitat Rain forests with high humidity; also enters houses

Distribution Southeastern Asia (India–Nicobar Islands–Myanmar, southern Thailand, Malaysian Peninsula, Borneo, Sumatra, and Java)

Status Common

Similar species Apart from 5 other species of flying geckos, the species is very distinctive

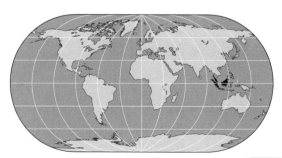

Golden-Tailed Gecko

Common name Golden-tailed gecko

Scientific name *Diplodactylus taenicauda*

Family Diplodactylidae

Suborder Sauria

Order Squamata

Size 4.7 in (12 cm) long

Key features Head and body gray and black with a network of fine gray lines enclosing black spots of varying sizes; a bright orange stripe runs along the top of the tail; eyes also bright orange; toes end in small pads consisting of a pair of rounded scales with a small claw positioned between them; hatchlings and juveniles lack bright orange markings

Habits Arboreal and nocturnal; active throughout the year, but very cold weather causes it to remain in hiding; capable of secreting foul-smelling fluid from pores in its tail when threatened

Breeding Female lays 2 parchment-shelled eggs; in captivity eggs hatch after 52–77 days

Diet Small invertebrates

Habitat Dry forests and sparse eucalyptus woodlands

Distribution Australia (eastern Queensland)

Status Common in suitable habitat

Similar species There are other *Diplodactylus* species with similar size and body shapes, but none has the distinctive markings of this species

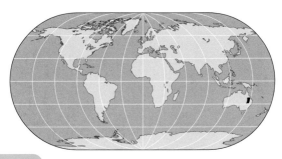

Northern Leaf-Tailed Gecko

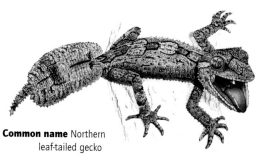

Common name Northern leaf-tailed gecko

Scientific name *Saltuarius cornutus* (previously *Phyllurus cornutus*)

Family Diplodactylidae

Suborder Sauria

Order Squamata

Size Up to 13 in (33 cm) long

Key features Body slender and flattened; head triangular; limbs and digits spindly; tail shaped like a leaf or shield with a short spike at the end; feet have claws but no toe pads; each flank has a fold and a series of frilly or spiny scales; color brown, gray, or olive with a row of large pale blotches down the back; can be very hard to see when resting on a lichen-covered branch or tree trunk

Habits Arboreal and nocturnal

Breeding Female lays 2 parchment-shelled eggs; further details unknown

Diet Invertebrates

Habitat Rain forests and wet temperate forests

Distribution Australia (northeastern Queensland)

Status Common

Similar species *Saltuarius saleborus* from the same region is almost indistinguishable but has rough scales on its throat and a longer spiny extension to the tail; there are 11 other leaf-tailed geckos, including several only recently described, but they have less flattened tails

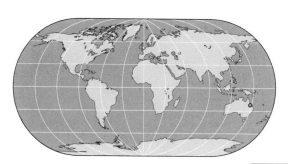

Flap-Footed Lizards

Common name Flap-footed lizards, scaly-footed lizards, snake lizards

Burton's snake lizard *(Lialis burtoni)*

Family Pygopodidae

Suborder Sauria

Order Squamata

Number of species 35

Size From 8 in (20 cm) to 30 in (76 cm) total length; average head and body length excluding tail from 3 in (7.6 cm) to 4.8 in (12 cm)

Key features Snakelike lizards with no visible limbs; some species have a small flap of skin in place of the hind legs; tail is at least as long as the head and body combined—often twice as long and occasionally 4 times as long—but regrown tails may be shorter; ear openings sometimes present; eyelids absent, and the lizards use their tongue to clean dust from their eyes

Habits Terrestrial and diurnal but secretive; often live in leaf litter

Breeding Egg layers; females produce 2 soft-shelled eggs; eggs hatch after 66–80 days in some species

Diet Insects, spiders, and scorpions; the snake lizards, *Lialis*, eat other lizards, especially skinks

Habitat Varied from open woodland and grassland to Mallee scrub and desert

Distribution Australia and southern New Guinea

Status Some species are extremely rare, possibly endangered; others can be fairly common in suitable habitat

Similar species None (other than snakes)

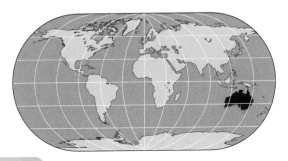

Granite Night Lizard

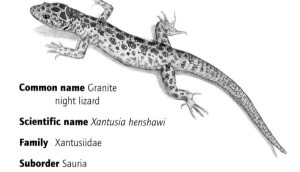

Common name Granite night lizard

Scientific name *Xantusia henshawi*

Family Xantusiidae

Suborder Sauria

Order Squamata

Size From 4 in (10 cm) to 5 in (13 cm) long

Key features A small, flattened lizard with smooth, shiny skin made up of a large number of small scales; eyes moderately large with vertical pupils but no movable eyelids; head wide and flattened and covered with large, symmetrical scales; markings consist of large dark-brown blotches separated by narrow white or yellow netting; limbs thin with long claws for climbing

Habits Very secretive; active in the evening

Breeding Female gives birth to 1–2 young in the fall; gestation period about 3 months

Diet Small invertebrates and some plant material

Habitat Rocky outcrops and hillsides in canyons, where it hides in crevices

Distribution Southern California and northern Baja California, Mexico

Status Common in suitable habitat

Similar species *Xantusia bezyi*, recently described from Arizona, is very similar, as is *X. bolsonae* from Durango, Mexico

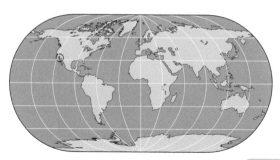

Bushveld Lizard

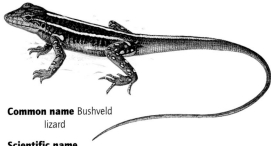

Common name Bushveld lizard

Scientific name *Heliobolus lugubris*

Family Lacertidae

Suborder Sauria

Order Squamata

Size 6 in (15 cm) long

Key features Typically lacertid in shape with a pointed snout, cylindrical body, and long limbs and tail; adults are light grayish brown or reddish brown in color with 3 pale cream stripes running down the back; only the center stripe continues onto the tail, which is brown; juveniles are completely different, black with white spots and a sandy-colored tail

Habits Terrestrial and diurnal

Breeding Female lays clutch of 4–6 eggs; eggs hatch after about 6 weeks

Diet Small insects, especially termites

Habitat Dry grassland and scrub

Distribution Southern Africa

Status Common in suitable habitat

Similar species The many African desert lacertids can be difficult to identify in the field; the bold stripes of this species are a good field mark, and juveniles are very distinctive; 2 other species in the genus occur farther north in East Africa; another occurs in West and Central Africa

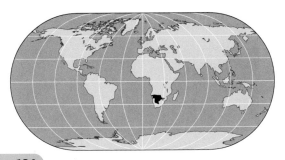

Eyed Lizard

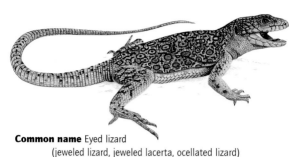

Common name Eyed lizard
(jeweled lizard, jeweled lacerta, ocellated lizard)

Scientific name *Lacerta lepida*

Family Lacertidae

Suborder Sauria

Order Squamata

Size From 24 in (60 cm) to 30 in (76 cm)

Key features A large lizard with a massive head, especially in
males; body only slightly flattened; tail thick at the base;
usually green on the back with black stippling and a
number of blue spots, or ocelli, on the sides; females are
more brownish green than males and have fewer blue
spots; spots may be absent altogether

Habits Terrestrial and diurnal

Breeding Female lays 4-6 eggs that hatch in 8-14 weeks;
occasionally lays a second clutch

Diet Almost anything; large insects, other lizards, snakes,
frogs, rodents, and nestling birds; also fruit and other
vegetation

Habitat Varied but usually dry hillsides, scrub, roadsides, olive
groves, vineyards

Distribution Iberian Peninsula, southern France, and extreme
northwestern Italy

Status Common but never in high densities

Similar species Green lizards, including *L. viridis*, and Schreiber's
lizard, *L. schreiberi*, are sometimes similar to small eyed
lizards, but they all lack the blue eyespots

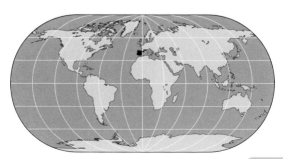

Viviparous Lizard

Common name
Viviparous lizard
(European common lizard)

Scientific name *Lacerta vivipara*

Family Lacertidae

Suborder Sauria

Order Squamata

Size 6 in (15 cm) long

Key features Small but robustly built with a cylindrical body, short legs, and a long tail; head short and deep with a rounded snout; neck thick; color and markings highly variable; most are some shade of brown but can also be olive or gray; females often have a plain back with a single dark stripe down the center and dark markings on the flanks; males are darker overall and have small markings consisting of light spots with black edges (ocelli); underside can be white, yellow, or orange

Habits Diurnal; mainly terrestrial

Breeding Most give birth to live young with litters of 3-11 born after a gestation of 8-13 weeks; some populations lay eggs

Diet Small invertebrates; also ants' eggs and larvae

Habitat Very adaptable but absent from forests, cultivated fields, and grazed meadows

Distribution Most of Europe except the Mediterranean region but including northern Spain east to north Asia as far as the Pacific coast and Sakhalin Island, Russia, and Hokkaido Island, Japan

Status Common in suitable habitat

Similar species All small lacertids are difficult to identify in the field, but the common lizard is usually darker than most; the others tend to have slightly flattened body shapes

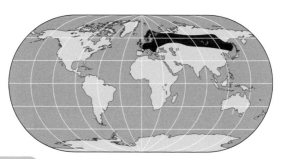

African Desert and Sand Lizards

Wedge-snouted sand lizard
(*Meroles cuneirostris*)

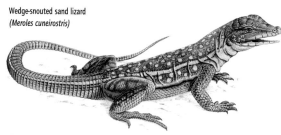

Common name African desert lizards, African sand lizards

Scientific name *Meroles* and *Pedioplanis*

Family Lacertidae

Suborder Sauria

Order Squamata

Number of species *Meroles* 7; *Pedioplanis* 10

Size From 6 in (15 cm) to 8 in (20 cm) long

Key features Slender, long-legged, long-tailed lizards with
pointed snouts that are often upturned slightly or wedge
shaped; color brown, reddish brown, or buff depending
on the surface on which they live, with lines and spots of
lighter and darker shades; desert lizards have fringes of
hairlike scales beneath their toes, but they are lacking in
the sand lizards

Habits Terrestrial and diurnal

Breeding Females lay clutches of up to 8 eggs that hatch after
about 60 days

Diet Insects, including beetles, grasshoppers, and locusts;
some species eat seeds

Habitat Rocky or sandy deserts

Distribution Southern Africa

Status Very common in suitable habitats

Similar species Sandveld lizards, *Nucras* sp.

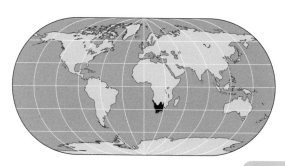

Wall Lizard

Common name Wall lizard

Scientific name *Podarcis muralis*

Family Lacertidae

Suborder Sauria

Order Squamata

Size 8.5 in (22 cm) long

Key features Graceful lizard with a narrow head, pointed snout, long tail, and relatively long limbs; coloration extremely variable, and many subspecies are recognized; some forms entirely brown with light and dark markings on their back and sides; in other places they are green (especially males) with extensive black markings; females usually have darker flanks than males and often have a line down the center of the back; markings of males are more likely to be netlike or scattered randomly

Habits Terrestrial and climbing; diurnal

Breeding Female lays clutches of 2-10 eggs that hatch after 6-11 weeks

Diet Insects and spiders

Habitat Dry, open places, including south-facing banks and rock faces, and stone walls around fields and the sides of buildings; often found in villages and the outskirts of larger towns

Distribution Europe from northern Spain and western France through Central Europe and northern Italy to the Peloponnese, Greece; also in Turkey.

Status Very common in suitable habitat

Similar species Many small lacertids from the region are similar and difficult to separate from the wall lizard and each other; locality is often the best means of identification

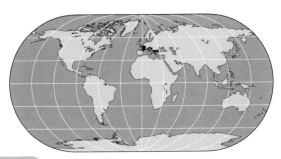

Large Sand Racer

Common name Large sand racer

Scientific name *Psammodromus algirus*

Family Lacertidae

Suborder Sauria

Order Squamata

Size 9 in (23 cm) long

Key features Typical lacertid shape with a long tail and limbs and narrow head; scales heavily keeled, overlapping, and ending in a point; tail can be up to 3 times as long as head and body combined, and is stiff; color midbrown with 2 yellowish stripes down the back and another down each flank; males may have blue eyespots at the base of their front legs; hatchlings have reddish flanks

Habits Terrestrial, climbing occasionally; diurnal

Breeding Female lays clutches of 2–11 eggs that hatch after 5-6 weeks

Diet Mainly small insects and spiders

Habitat Dry, scrubby, or bushy places; often lives around the base of heather, gorse, and other dense bushes; rarely ventures into the open

Distribution Most of Spain and Portugal extending along the Mediterranean coast of France; also North Africa

Status Common but often overlooked

Similar species The Spanish sand racer, *P. hispanicus*, is smaller and has spots or dashes on its back rather than stripes

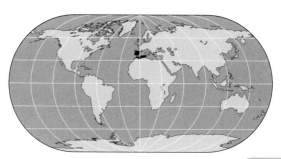

Six-Lined Grass Lizard

Common name Six-lined grass lizard

Scientific name *Takydromus sexlineatus*

Family Lacertidae

Suborder Sauria

Order Squamata

Size 14 in (36 cm) long, of which up to 80 percent is the tail

Key features Head and body typical of many lacertids but slightly flattened and elongated; however, limbs are short; tail extremely elongated; scales large, keeled, and prominent; keels are aligned and form continuous ridges down the body; basic color brown with white or yellow flanks and a number (not necessarily 6) of light stripes down the back; stripes sometimes green in males, but females are less colorful

Habits Diurnal and terrestrial; climbs only occasionally

Breeding Female lays small clutches of eggs, but details are lacking

Diet Insects and spiders

Habitat Grassland; found in a variety of places wherever there is a good covering of grasses

Distribution Asia (India, China, Myanmar, Thailand, Indochina, Malaysia, and Indonesia)

Status Common

Similar species There are 21 other species in the genus, all with similar body plans; *T. sexlineatus*, however, has the largest range and is the most common species over much of the region

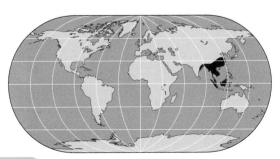

Jungle Racer

Common name Jungle racer
(common ameiva)

Scientific name *Ameiva ameiva*

Family Teiidae

Suborder Sauria

Order Squamata

Size From 16 in (41 cm) to 24 in (60 cm) long

Key features Body stocky; head deep, pointed, and angular and
covered in large scales; limbs long; claws also long,
especially on hind legs; tail cylindrical and accounts for
just over half the total length if it is complete; body
scales small and granular; color mainly brown with some
areas of green on the back; a pattern of light and dark
spots appears on the flanks, often arranged into vague
cross-bands

Habits Terrestrial and diurnal

Breeding Female lays clutches of 2–9 eggs; further details
unknown

Diet Insects and small vertebrates, including other lizards

Habitat In clearings and on paths and roadsides in otherwise
forested areas

Distribution Northern South America from Panama throughout
the Amazon Basin to northern Argentina

Status Common

Similar species There are over 30 other *Ameiva* species and 9
Kentropyx species, all of which look quite similar; the
jungle racer is larger than most, is the most widespread,
and the one most likely to be seen

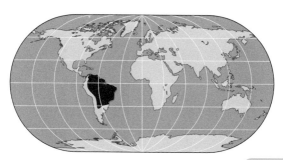

Desert Grassland Whiptail

Common name Desert grassland whiptail

Scientific name *Cnemidophorus uniparens*

Family Teiidae

Suborder Sauria

Order Squamata

Size 9 in (23 cm) long

Key features A small, graceful lizard with a long cylindrical body; long tail accounts for about two-thirds of total length if complete; head narrow and pointed; limbs long, especially the back ones, which also have long toes; color rich brown with 6 unbroken cream stripes from the back of the head to the base of the tail; juveniles have blue tails

Habits Terrestrial and diurnal

Breeding Parthenogenetic; females lay 1–4 eggs without the help of males; eggs hatch into more females in 50–55 days

Diet Insects and spiders

Habitat Dry scrub and grassland; open forests in mountain foothills

Distribution North America (southeastern Arizona, southwestern New Mexico, and adjacent parts of Mexico to the south)

Status Common

Similar species Other whiptails, of which there are a number in the region

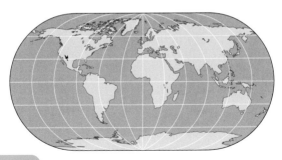

Caiman Lizard

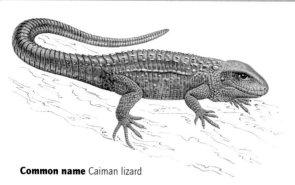

Common name Caiman lizard

Scientific name *Dracaena guianensis*

Family Teiidae

Suborder Sauria

Order Squamata

Size From 36 in (91 cm) to 42 in (107 cm) long

Key features A very distinctive lizard; body stocky; head large; large studlike scales present on the neck; numerous raised keels on the back are arranged into rough lines; keels on the tail form a pair of saw-tooth crests; body color bright green, olive, or brown; head orange

Habits Semiaquatic; diurnal

Breeding Female lays clutches consisting of 2 eggs

Diet Mostly aquatic snails

Habitat Amazonian forest in swamps, along riversides, and in flooded areas

Distribution South America (Amazon Basin)

Status Rarely seen, probably because its preferred habitat is difficult to explore

Similar species There is another caiman lizard, *D. paraguayensis*, farther south

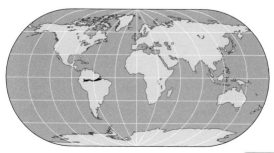

Tegu

Common name Tegu (black-and-white tegu)

Scientific name *Tupinambis teguixin*

Family Teiidae

Suborder Sauria

Order Squamata

Size To 43 in (109 cm), of which just under half is the tail

Key features Large and powerful lizard with a cylindrical body; tail thick; head long; snout narrow; limbs are also powerful and end in long claws; the whole lizard is covered with small shiny scales that give it a glossy appearance; adults boldly marked in black and white or black and yellow, but juveniles are bright green

Habits Terrestrial and diurnal

Breeding Female lays 7–30 eggs that hatch after about 12 weeks

Diet Insects, spiders, other lizards, birds and their eggs, small mammals; also eats carrion

Habitat Rain forests in clearings and along river courses

Distribution South America (Brazil, Peru, Colombia, Venezuela, Ecuador, northern Argentina, Uruguay, Bolivia, Guyana, Surinam, French Guyana); Trinidad

Status Common in suitable habitat, although never in large numbers

Similar species Up to 6 other species in the genus occur throughout South America, all differing slightly in coloration, but the validity of some is in doubt; otherwise there are no similar species; juveniles could possibly be mistaken for jungle racers, *Ameiva* species

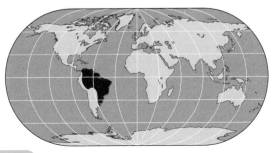

Black Girdle-Tailed Lizard

Common name
Black girdle-tailed lizard

Scientific name *Cordylus niger*

Family Cordylidae

Suborder Sauria

Order Squamata

Size 6 in (15 cm) long

Key features Body flattened, head flat and triangular and covered with smooth shields; scales around the back of the head are smooth and do not end in spines; scales on the back are only slightly keeled but more heavily keeled along the centerline; tail spiny; both sexes as well as juveniles are completely black in color and only slightly paler beneath

Habits Diurnal and rock dwelling (saxicolous)

Breeding Live-bearer; female has litter of 1–3 large young

Diet Insects and spiders

Habitat Rock outcrops in the coastal scrub known as fynbos

Distribution South Africa; occurs only in a small area consisting of the Cape Peninsula and on coastal rocks farther north

Status Common in suitable habitat but with a limited range; protected (CITES Appendix II)

Similar species The only other black species in the same area is Oelofsen's girdle-tailed lizard, *C. oelofseni*, but dark or black species live elsewhere, especially in coastal regions

Armadillo Lizard

Common name Armadillo lizard

Scientific name *Cordylus cataphractus*

Family Cordylidae

Suborder Sauria

Order Squamata

Size 7 in (18 cm) long; males are slightly larger than females

Key features Body flattened; head flat, wide, and triangular, fringed with backward-pointing spiny scales; scales on the back are very large, with only 15–17 rows between the neck and the base of the tail; each scale is keeled and ends in a small spine; tail is ringed with large spiny scales; back is pale brown with no markings; underside of the throat and body are yellowish

Habits Diurnal and rock dwelling (saxicolous)

Breeding Live-bearer; female has litter of 1 or 2 young

Diet Insects

Habitat Rocky places

Distribution Southwest South Africa

Status Becoming rare

Similar species Other girdle-tailed lizards usually have smaller scales on their back, although confusion is possible with other brown species, such as the Namaqua girdle-tailed lizard, *C. namaquensis*, especially at a distance

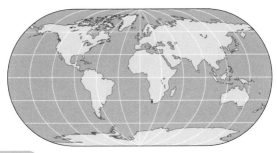

Broadley's Flat Lizard

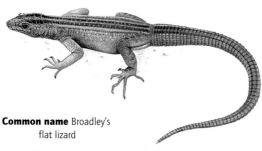

Common name Broadley's flat lizard

Scientific name *Platysaurus broadleyi*

Family Cordylidae

Suborder Sauria

Order Squamata

Size 6 in (15 cm) long

Key features Head and body are wafer thin; back is covered with fine, granular scales, but the head has large platelike scales; males are spectacular with blue head, greenish back, and orange or yellow front legs; throat and chest in males is electric blue, and the belly is glossy black; females and juveniles are brown with 3 wide cream stripes running down the back

Habits Diurnal and rock dwelling (saxicolous)

Breeding Egg layer; female lays 2 elongated eggs in rock crevices

Diet Mainly insects, especially flies, but also some plant material

Habitat Granite rock outcrops

Distribution Limited to the area around the lower Orange River in the vicinity of Augrabies Falls, South Africa

Status Very numerous over a small area

Similar species All flat lizards are similar, but the markings of males vary slightly; their ranges do not overlap, so they are easily identified by locality

Cape Crag Lizard

Common name Cape crag lizard

Scientific name *Pseudocordylus microlepidotus*

Family Cordylidae

Suborder Sauria

Order Squamata

Size 10 in (25 cm) long

Key features A large crag lizard with a large head and bulges on its cheeks due to its powerful jaw muscles; the scales on the back are smaller than those of girdle-tailed lizards but still arranged in regular rows; each large scale is surrounded by a number of small granular scales; limbs are well developed; tail is ringed with spiny scales; males have reddish-brown back with yellow or orange crossbars; flanks and underside of body and limbs are also yellow or orange in males

Habits Diurnal and rock dwelling (saxicolous)

Breeding Live-bearer; female has litter of 3–7 young

Diet Large grasshoppers, crickets, and beetles; occasionally small lizards

Habitat Rocky, vegetated hills and mountainsides

Distribution Southern parts of South Africa on inland mountain ranges

Status Common

Similar species The graceful crag lizard, *P. capensis*, lives in part of the range, but it is smaller, more dainty, and lives on steeper rock faces

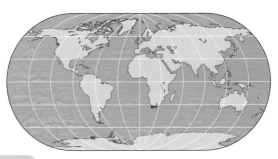

Giant Plated Lizard

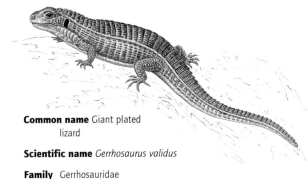

Common name Giant plated lizard

Scientific name *Gerrhosaurus validus*

Family Gerrhosauridae

Suborder Sauria

Order Squamata

Size 14 in (36 cm) long

Key features A large lizard with a flattened body and head; tail long, often thickened at the base; legs well developed but short; body scales rectangular and arranged in regular rows; an obvious fold present down each side of the body; adults are dark brown, but each scale on the head and back has a small yellow spot, creating a speckled appearance; some have a pair of cream stripes on the back; juveniles are dark brown with larger yellow spots on their back and crossbars on their flanks

Habits Diurnal and terrestrial

Breeding Female lays clutch of 2–5 eggs in rock crevice

Diet Invertebrates, small vertebrates, and some vegetable material

Habitat Grassland, mainly on rocky slopes or well-vegetated rock outcrops

Distribution Eastern subspecies, *G. v. validus*, occurs from northeast South Africa through Zimbabwe and Mozambique to Malawi and Zambia; western subspecies, *G. v. maltzahni*, lives in Namibia

Status Common in suitable habitat

Similar species The rough-scaled plated lizard, *G. major*, is the other large species, but it has heavily keeled scales and is pale brown in color, sometimes with a stripe down either side of its back

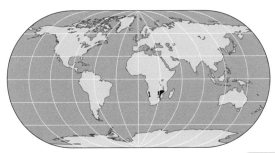

Monkey-Tailed Skink

Common name
Monkey-tailed
skink (zebra skink, Solomon Islands great skink)

Scientific name *Corucia zebrata*

Family Scincidae

Suborder Sauria

Order Squamata

Size Up to 30 in (76 cm) long

Key features Head large; body stout and long with well-developed limbs and sharp claws; tail long and prehensile; color olive-green to grayish green with mottling; eyes green or brown but yellow in the subspecies *C. z. alfred schmidti*

Habits Arboreal; crepuscular or nocturnal; spends days in tree hollows; lives in small groups or colonies of several females and their offspring and 1 adult male

Breeding Usually biennial; 1 or occasionally 2 live young produced after gestation lasting 7 months

Diet Plants, including *Piper* species and *Epipremnum pinnatum* (family Araceae); some fruit also eaten

Habitat Primary rain forest with high humidity, especially areas where strangler fig tree is prevalent

Distribution Solomon Islands

Status Vulnerable (IUCN)

Similar species None

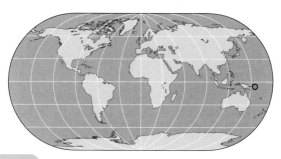

Three-Toed Skink

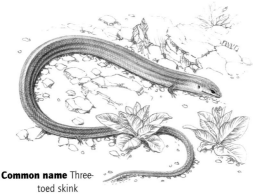

Common name Three-toed skink
(seps, barrel skink, cylindrical skink)

Scientific name *Chalcides chalcides*

Family Scincidae

Order Squamata

Size Up to 17 in (43 cm) long

Key features Body extremely elongated; color varies from olive-green to bronze, may be uniform or have dark, longitudinal lines; lower eyelids undivided with transparent disk; head conical; snout blunt; ear openings larger than nostrils; limbs and digits considerably reduced; 3 digits on each foot; tail 1–1.5 times the length of the body

Habits Diurnal or crepuscular depending on season; hibernates for 4–5 months; basks to raise body temperature before foraging for food

Breeding Live-bearer; female gives birth to 3–15 live young; gestation period 3–4 months

Diet Insects, spiders, caterpillars, centipedes

Habitat Moist, grassy areas to drier, stony regions

Distribution Italy, southern France, Iberia, North Africa

Status Common

Similar species *Chalcides mionecton; C. sepsoides*

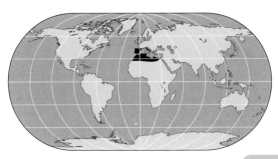

Spiny-Tailed Skink

Common name Spiny-tailed
skink (Stokes's skink, Gidgee skink)

Scientific name *Egernia stokesii*

Family Scincidae

Suborder Sauria

Order Squamata

Size 10 in (25 cm) long

Key features Medium-sized skink with flattened body and tail;
tail relatively short and sharply tapering; 2 spines
present on each keeled dorsal scale, 1 large spine on
each tail scale; color and markings vary according to
location, may be reddish brown to dark brown with pale
or dark blotches or bands

Habits Terrestrial, living in crevices or under rock formations in
colonies; diurnal, quite secretive

Breeding Live-bearer; female gives birth to 5–6 young; gestation
period 4 months

Diet Range of insects and plant material

Habitat Rocky areas in dry to semiarid regions with tree scrub
cover and *Acacia*

Distribution Western and central Australia; various islands off
the coast of Western Australia

Status *E. s. badia*—Endangered (IUCN); *E. s. stokesii*—Vulnerable
(IUCN)

Similar species The pygmy spiny-tailed skink, *E. depressa*, but
that species has 3 spines on each tail scale

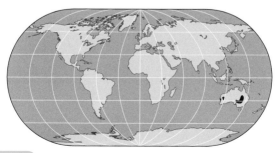

Five-Lined Skink

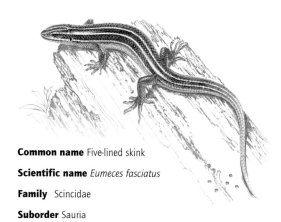

Common name Five-lined skink

Scientific name *Eumeces fasciatus*

Family Scincidae

Suborder Sauria

Order Squamata

Size Up to 8 in (20 cm) long

Key features Body slender and elongated; body color tan, bronze, or grayish olive-green with pale stripes; juveniles have 5 longitudinal bright-cream to yellow stripes on a black background; tail is blue in juveniles and some females but fades to gray in adult males; head wedge shaped; ear opening distinct; limbs short, each bearing 5 digits with claws; scales smooth

Habits Diurnal; terrestrial; may climb onto tree stumps to bask and look for insects; also burrows under rocks

Breeding Egg layer; clutch containing 4–15 eggs laid in a nest dug in moist soil; eggs hatch after 33–35 days

Diet Insects, spiders, earthworms, crustaceans, and small lizards

Habitat Humid woods with leaf litter and tree stumps; may also be seen around human habitations

Distribution Southern New England to northern Florida west to Texas, Kansas, Wisconsin, and southern Ontario; isolated groups may occur farther west

Status Common but listed as being of special concern in some parts of its range, e.g., Iowa

Similar species *Eumeces inexpectatus* and *E. laticeps* have similar colors and longitudinal stripes

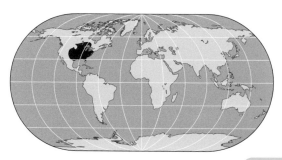

Berber Skink

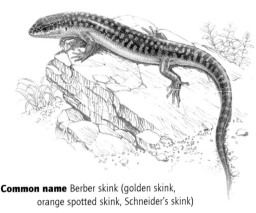

Common name Berber skink (golden skink, orange spotted skink, Schneider's skink)

Scientific name *Eumeces schneideri*

Family Scincidae

Suborder Sauria

Order Squamata

Size Up to 18 in (46 cm) long

Key features Head triangular shaped with pointed snout; eyes relatively large; body long and cylindrical with overlapping smooth scales; tail long and tapering; 4 well-developed limbs each with 5 long digits; basic dorsal color brownish or greenish gray; yellow-orange transverse stripes present on males and occasionally on females

Habits Terrestrial and burrowing; most of the time spent foraging on the ground but capable of disappearing beneath the surface or into water when danger is spotted

Breeding Female lays clutches of 3–20 eggs that hatch after 5–6 weeks

Diet Insects, sometimes small lizards

Habitat Variable, ranging from moist, grassy areas to semidesert

Distribution Northern Africa to Central Asia

Status Common

Similar species The Algerian skink, *E. algeriensis*, but it lacks the lateral yellow-orange stripe

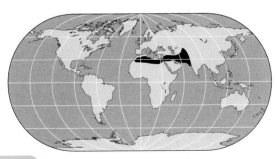

Cape Skink

Common name Cape skink

Scientific name *Mabuya capensis*

Family Scincidae

Suborder Sauria

Order Squamata

Size From 8 in (20 cm) to 10 in (25 cm) long

Key features Head with pointed snout; movable eyelid has large, transparent window; ear opening visible; body heavy; background color light brown to olive- or grayish brown with 3 pale stripes and cream and dark brown or black spots between the stripes; underside white or light gray; scales are cycloid (almost circular) and keeled; tail slightly longer than head and body length combined; spiny scales on soles of feet; females larger than males

Habits Terrestrial and diurnal; digs tunnels at the base of shrubs; basks in open areas

Breeding In most of the range females give birth to 5–18 live young after gestation period of 4 months; in 2 areas females lay a clutch of 6–12 eggs that hatch after about 2 months

Diet Insects, beetles, spiders, and worms

Habitat Very varied, including moist coastal bush, grassland, karroid veldt, and suburban gardens

Distribution Most of southern Africa except the Namib Desert and extreme northern regions

Status Common

Similar species Variable skink, *M. varia*, has individuals that also lay eggs or give birth to live young depending on distribution and altitude

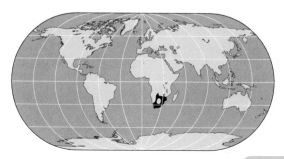

Blind Burrowing Skinks

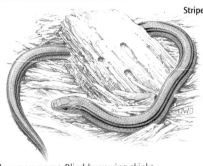

Striped blind legless skink
(*Typhlosaurus
lineatus*)

Common name Blind burrowing skinks

Scientific name *Typhlosaurus* sp.

Family Scincidae

Suborder Sauria

Order Squamata

Size From 4.8 in (12 cm) to 12.6 in (32 cm) long

Number of species About 9

Key features Body long and thin with smooth scales; limbs
lacking; large rostral scale on head; vestigial eyes
present under head shields; no external ear openings;
some species are light pink in color with a translucent
underside; others are usually orange or golden yellow
with stripes

Habits Burrowing and subterranean; spend most of the time
below ground or under rocks and fallen logs; usually
emerge only at night

Breeding 2 species are live-bearers producing 1 or 2 young;
1 species is an egg layer producing clutches of 3 eggs

Diet Termites and beetle larvae

Habitat Semiarid areas with sand dunes or sandy soils and
sparse vegetation

Distribution Transvaal, Zimbabwe, eastern Cape, Mozambique,
Namib Desert, Botswana, Namaqualand; 1 species found
in Zambia

Status Locally common, but *T. lomii* is Vulnerable (IUCN)

Similar species Giant legless skinks, *Acontias* sp.

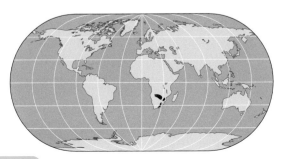

Fire Skink

Common name Fire skink (common fire skink, Fernand's fire skink, Togo fire skink)

Scientific name *Riopa fernandi*

Family Scincidae

Suborder Sauria

Order Squamata

Size Up to 14 in (36 cm) long

Key features Body cylindrical; limbs reduced; tail relatively long; blunt-shaped head; back bronze with red-and-black sides; throat and tail are black with white speckles; juveniles are black with red-and-gold markings, and their tail is black with contrasting light-blue rings

Habits Active by day; spends most of the time foraging in leaf litter or constructing series of tunnels

Breeding Female lays 3 to 4 clutches containing 4–9 eggs that hatch after about 65–75 days

Diet Insects, beetles, and spiders

Habitat Equatorial rain forests and plantations

Distribution West Africa (Cameroon, Togo, Equatorial Guinea, Nigeria, Ghana)

Status Common

Similar species *Riopa sundevalli*

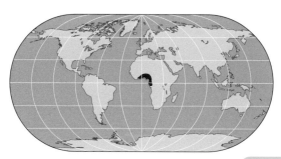

Sandfish

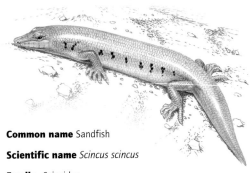

Common name Sandfish

Scientific name *Scincus scincus*

Family Scincidae

Suborder Sauria

Order Squamata

Size 8.8 in (22 cm) long

Key features Head flattened; snout wedge shaped with countersunk jaw; scales smooth; toes have spadelike protruberances that act like flippers; tail laterally compressed and shorter than combined head and body length; color in adults yellow to brownish tan with yellow or brown spots or streaks and gray to tan transverse bands; juveniles are usually a uniform salmon color with a silvery-white underside

Habits Diurnal, changing to nocturnal during the hottest months; hibernates in winter; basks with its whole body or just the head exposed depending on the time of day

Breeding Female lays 1 clutch of 6 eggs at night in moist, sandy areas; eggs hatch after about 2 months

Diet Locusts, ants, spiders, beetles, small lizards, insects, some vegetable matter

Habitat Compacted and loose sand with vegetation

Distribution Northern Africa from southern Tunisia to Egypt to the Mediterranean coast; also in parts of Israel, Jordan, Iran, Iraq, and Saudi Arabia

Status Common

Similar species *Scincus mitranus*; the Senegal skink, *S. albifasciatus*

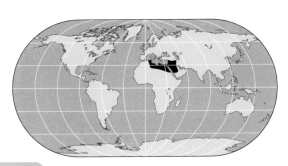

Blue-Tongued Skink

Common name
Blue-tongued skink

Scientific name *Tiliqua scincoides*

Family Scincidae

Suborder Sauria

Order Squamata

Size Up to 24 in (60 cm) long

Key features Head large; lower eyelid movable without a transparent window; body stout and flattened across the back from side to side; scales smooth; limbs relatively short but well developed; color varies according to subspecies, usually gray to tan or silver background with bands extending onto the sides; some have a dark streak running from the eye to the top of the ear opening; tongue blue

Habits Diurnal ground dweller, usually slow moving; spends a lot of time basking and foraging for food

Breeding Live-bearer; female gives birth to up to 25 young; gestation period about 110 days

Diet Omnivorous; eats insects, fruit, berries, flowers, even carrion

Habitat Temperate forests, subhumid forests, grassland, suburban gardens

Distribution Eastern and northern Australia and Irian Jaya (Indonesia)

Status Common

Similar species Centralian blue-tongued skink, *T. multifasciata*; western blue-tongued skink, *T. occipitalis*; blotched blue-tongued skink, *T. nigrolutea*; pygmy blue-tongued skink, *T. adelaidensis*; New Guinea blue-tongued skink, *T. gigas*

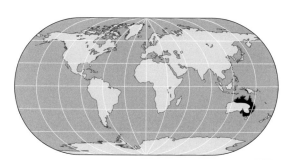

Stump-Tailed Skink

Common name Stump-tailed skink (Boggi, sleepy lizard, pine-cone lizard, bob-tailed lizard, shingleback lizard)

Scientific name *Trachydosaurus rugosus*

Family Scincidae

Suborder Sauria

Order Squamata

Size From 16 in (41 cm) to 18 in (46 cm) long

Key features Heavy bodied with triangular-shaped head; ear openings conspicuous; legs noticeably reduced; toes short; tail blunt and short and resembles head; scales large, rough, knobby; tongue blue; body color and pattern vary with location, can be uniform dark brown or black or have contrasting bands or flecks of white, yellow, or gray

Habits Basks early in the day to raise temperature, followed by periods of feeding; retreats to shelter toward the end of the day

Breeding Live-bearer; female produces 1 or 2 young; gestation period 5 months

Diet Omnivorous; mainly plant and vegetable matter supplemented with insects, snails, and carrion

Habitat Semiarid plains and drier woodlands

Distribution Southern Australia from New South Wales to the coast of Western Australia; also Rottnest Island off the coast of Western Australia

Status Locally common

Similar species None

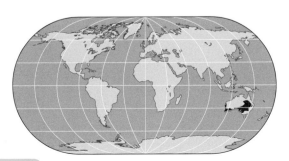

Crocodile Skink

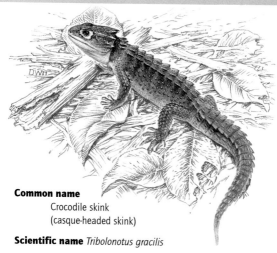

Common name
Crocodile skink
(casque-headed skink)

Scientific name *Tribolonotus gracilis*

Family Scincidae

Suborder Sauria

Order Squamata

Size 8 in (20 cm)

Key features Head triangular shaped with casque at rear; body
scales large and spiny; scales on tail point backward;
body color brown on the back with a yellowish-brown
underside; orange ring surrounds most of the eye; yellow
pigment present on anterior edge of the eye

Habits Mainly active at dusk; semiburrower, spends much of the
time in leaf litter or under foliage on banks of streams

Breeding Egg layer; female lays 1 (occasionally 2) eggs that
hatch after 65–75 days; several clutches laid in a season

Diet Omnivorous

Habitat Forest and coconut plantations close to water

Distribution New Guinea

Status Vulnerable (IUCN)

Similar species *Tribolonotus novaeguineae*

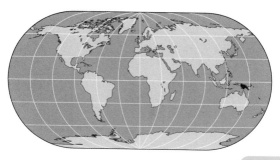

Slow Worm

Common name Slow worm (blind worm)

Scientific name *Anguis fragilis*

Subfamily Anguinae

Family Anguidae

Suborder Sauria

Order Squamata

Size Up to 20 in (51 cm) long but usually shorter

Key features Legless lizard; scales smooth and shiny; head no wider than its body; no distinct neck region; eyes small; tail longer than body when complete; color brown, sometimes coppery; females have a thin dark line down the center of the back and dark flanks; males usually uniform in color; juveniles look like females but are often more brightly colored

Habits Terrestrial; semiburrowing; active at night; occasionally basks in the day

Breeding Live-bearer; female gives birth to 6–12 young; gestation period 8–12 weeks

Diet Soft-bodied invertebrates, especially small slugs, snails, and worms; insects and small lizards

Habitat Damp places with plenty of vegetation, including woodland clearings, hedges, banks, gardens, parks, and railway embankments

Distribution Most of Europe except the southern half of Spain and the most northerly parts of Scandinavia; east Asia to west Siberia, the Caucasus, northern Turkey, northwest Iran

Status Common

Similar species Young European glass lizards, *Ophisaurus apodus*, but they are spotted; snakes are more supple, lack eyelids, and have a single row of wide scales down the belly

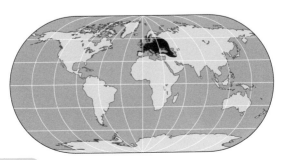

Eastern Glass Lizard

Common name Eastern glass lizard (Florida glass lizard)

Scientific name *Ophisaurus ventralis*

Subfamily Anguinae

Family Anguidae

Suborder Sauria

Order Squamata

Size 39 in (99 cm) long

Key features A stiff, legless lizard with eyelids and external ear openings; a groove along its side marks the change from grayish-brown flanks with white bars to the plain, off-white underside; the back is plain brown in color; side of the head is marked with dark-edged, whitish bars, but they may disappear with age

Habits Diurnal; terrestrial

Breeding Female lays 8–17 eggs that hatch after 8–9 weeks

Diet Invertebrates, especially slugs, snails, and earthworms

Habitat Grassland, open woods, fields, and parks

Distribution Southeastern United States (North Carolina, the whole of Florida, eastern Louisiana)

Status Common

Similar species The ranges of 3 other glass lizards—the slender, the island, and the mimic (*O. attenuatus*, *O. compressus*, and *O. mimicus*)—overlap the range of the eastern glass lizard; the first 2 usually have some black striping along their back or flanks, while the mimic glass lizard is much smaller, about 15 in (38 cm) long

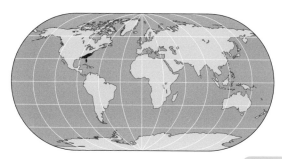

LIZARDS

European Glass Lizard

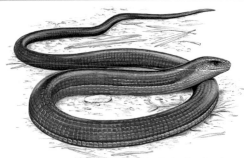

Common name European glass lizard (Pallas's glass lizard, *scheltopusik*)

Scientific name *Ophisaurus apodus*

Subfamily Anguinae

Family Anguidae

Suborder Sauria

Order Squamata

Size Up to 4.6 ft (1.4 m) long

Key features Effectively legless, although reduced legs are present in the form of small, flipperlike flaps of skin on either side of the cloaca; body thick; tail accounts for about two-thirds of the total length; it has eyelids and small external ear openings; scales arranged in regular rows across and down the body; a fold of skin runs along the sides; color uniform brown, paler on the underside; juveniles are gray with irregular brown blotches and crossbars

Habits Terrestrial; diurnal

Breeding Female lays 6–10 eggs that hatch after 45–55 days

Diet Mostly invertebrates, especially snails, and occasional small vertebrates such as mice

Habitat Dry, rocky hillsides, sparse woodlands, fields, and meadows

Distribution Southeast Europe, the Caucasus, and part of the Crimean Peninsula

Status Very common in suitable habitat

Similar species Unlikely to be confused with any other reptile in the region

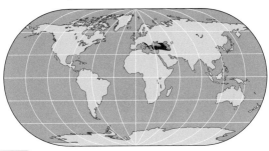

North American Legless Lizards

Anniella geronomensis

Common name Baja California legless lizard; California legless lizard

Scientific name *Anniella geronomensis* and *A. pulchra*

Subfamily Anniellinae

Family Anguidae

Suborder Sauria

Order Squamata

Size From 6 in (15 cm) to 7 in (18 cm) long

Key features Small legless lizards with few distinguishing marks; head small and pointed (when seen from the side) and not distinct from the neck; lower jaw deeply countersunk; eyes also sunk within the head and reduced to narrow horizontal slits; *A. geronomensis* is coppery or silvery brown in color with 7 or 8 thin black stripes running the length of the body; *A. pulchra* is similar but has 1 black line along the center of its back, another along each flank, and its underside is yellow

Habits Burrowers; sometimes bask on dunes but avoid extreme temperatures by moving around

Breeding Poorly known; may give birth to 1 or 2 live young in late summer or early fall

Diet Small invertebrates

Habitat Sand dunes (*A. geronomensis*); sandy soils (*A. pulchra*)

Distribution Baja California, Mexico (*A. geronomensis*), southern California (*A. pulchra*)

Status Probably common in suitable habitat but localized and hard to find

Similar species None in the region

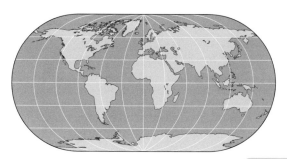

Giant Galliwasps

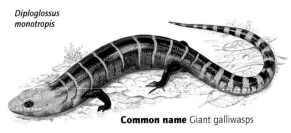

*Diploglossus
monotropis*

Common name Giant galliwasps

Scientific name *Celestus* and *Diploglossus*

Subfamily Diploglossinae

Family Anguidae

Suborder Sauria

Order Squamata

Size Body length over 12 in (30 cm); up to 18 in (46 cm) including tail

Key features Bulky, skinklike lizards with thick bodies, short limbs, and pointed snouts; heads covered with large, platelike scales; body scales shiny and overlapping with a rounded edge (cycloid); they have parallel ridges running down them (striations) that are better defined on some species than others; coloration varies, but most are shades of brown with orange or yellow markings; male *D. monotropis* are brightly marked in orange and yellow

Habits Diurnal or nocturnal depending on species; ground dwellers or semiburrowers

Breeding *Celestus* sp. are live-bearers; *Diploglossus* sp. may be live-bearers or egg layers; related species of egg-laying *Diploglossus* apparently coil around their incubating eggs

Diet Poorly known; large species are thought to be partly herbivorous; *C. occiduus* is reported to eat fish

Habitat Rain forests (among leaf litter) and swamps

Distribution Central America (*D. monotropis*) and the West Indies (Jamaica and Hispaniola)

Status Extremely rare, some possibly extinct

Similar species None in the region

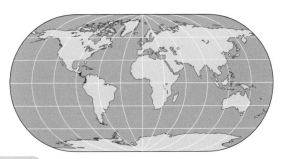

Southern Alligator Lizard

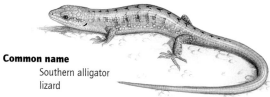

Common name
Southern alligator lizard

Scientific name *Elgaria multicarinata*

Subfamily Gerrhonotinae

Family Anguidae

Suborder Sauria

Order Squamata

Size From 10 in (25 cm) to 16 in (41 cm) long

Key features A large lizard with a wide, triangular head covered with large scales; forelimbs small; hind limbs slightly larger; a fold runs along each flank between the fore- and hind limbs; scales on its back and flanks are roughly square and keeled, giving it a ridged appearance; color reddish brown or tan on the back fading to grayish on the flanks, usually with irregular black bands

Habits Diurnal; semiarboreal

Breeding Female lays 2–3 clutches of eggs each year

Diet Insects and spiders; occasional small lizards, nestling birds and mice; also eats carrion

Habitat Moist grasslands and woodlands, especially in foothills

Distribution Western North America (southern Washington State south to Baja California along a fairly narrow coastal belt)

Status Common

Similar species Several other alligator lizards live in the same region; the northern alligator lizard, *E. coerulea*, is slightly smaller and has a more speckled pattern

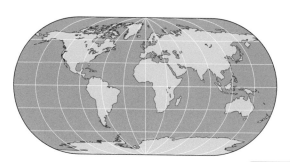

Chinese Crocodile Lizard

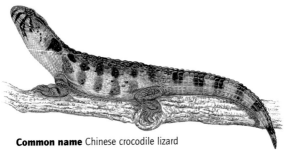

Common name Chinese crocodile lizard

Scientific name *Shinisaurus crocodilurus*

Family Xenosauridae

Suborder Sauria

Order Squamata

Size 16 in (41 cm) long

Key features Top of head flat; raised crest present above the eye and down the back; scales all of the same size and supported by bony plates beneath the skin; legs short and sturdy; claws strong; back and tail brown with yellow to orange underside; males larger than females and more brightly colored with orange sides and throat

Habits Diurnal; spends much of the day motionless in a pool or on a branch in the shade and overhanging water

Breeding Live-bearer; female produces up to 12 live young after a gestation period of 10–14 months

Diet Beetles, insects, fish, crustaceans, slugs, small frogs, tadpoles, and dragonfly larvae

Habitat Cloud forest with dense vegetation and small pools or slow-running rivulets

Distribution Kueilin and Kwangsi Province, China

Status Vulnerable (IUCN); Listed in CITES Appendix II; also protected locally

Similar species None

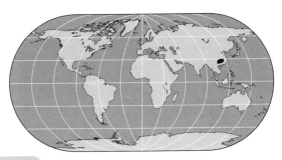

Gila Monster

Common name Gila monster (Aztec lizard)

Scientific name *Heloderma suspectum*

Family Helodermatidae

Suborder Sauria

Order Squamata

Size From 13 in (33 cm) to 22 in (56 cm) long

Key features Head rounded and bears a patch of light-colored scales; nose blunt; neck short; body heavy with short, powerful limbs and long claws; tail short and fat; scales beadlike; eyelids movable; camouflage colors of black, orange, yellow, and pink on the body; has 2 elongated cloacal scales

Habits Active by day, at dusk, or at night depending on season and temperatures; spends much of the time in burrows or in shaded areas

Breeding Female lays 1 clutch of up to 12 eggs in late summer; eggs hatch 10 months later

Diet Small mammals, eggs of birds and reptiles, insects

Habitat Dry grassland, deserts, and foothills of mountains

Distribution Southwestern United States and northwestern Mexico

Status Vulnerable (IUCN); listed in CITES Appendix II

Similar species The Mexican beaded lizard, *H. horridum*

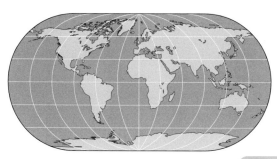

Mexican Beaded Lizard

Common name Mexican beaded lizard

Scientific name *Heloderma horridum*

Family Helodermatidae

Suborder Sauria

Order Squamata

Size Up to 35 in (89 cm) long

Key features Head rounded; nose blunt; neck quite long; body heavily built; limbs short with long claws on ends of digits; tail long; scales beadlike; eyelids movable; color variable according to subspecies, usually some shade of brown with yellow or cream markings; adults of 1 subspecies totally black

Habits Diurnal and nocturnal depending on the weather; also climbs trees; during hot weather spends much of daytime in rocky crevices and self-dug or preexisting burrows

Breeding Female lays 1 clutch of 7–10 eggs that hatch after 6 months

Diet Eggs of reptiles and birds, nestlings, small mammals, occasionally lizards

Habitat Edges of desert, thorn scrub, deciduous woodland

Distribution Western Mexico and Guatemala

Status Vulnerable (IUCN); listed in CITES Appendix II; also protected locally

Similar species The Gila monster, *H. suspectum*

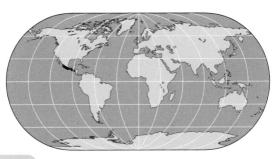

Ridge-Tailed Monitor

Common name Ridge-tailed monitor
(spiny-tailed monitor)

Scientific name *Varanus acanthurus*

Family Varanidae

Suborder Sauria

Order Squamata

Size 30 in (76 cm) long

Key features Body stocky with short legs; head long with
pointed snout; tail very spiny and round in cross-section;
color variable from black to brown to red

Habits Spends much of the day sitting on rocks, basking and
foraging among rocks for food; retreats under boulders
at night

Breeding Female lays 2–3 clutches of 2–11 eggs that hatch
after about 86–92 days

Diet Mainly insects and some small lizards

Habitat Rocky areas in tropical and subtropical habitats

Distribution Northern half of Australia (excluding Cape York
Peninsula) and islands off the northern and western
coasts

Status Common

Similar species The pygmy ridge-tailed monitor, *V. storri*, the
short-tailed monitor, *V. brevicauda*, and the northern
blunt-spined monitor, *V. primordius*

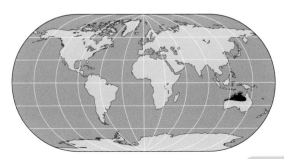

Bengal or Indian Monitor

Common name Bengal monitor (Indian monitor)

Scientific name *Varanus bengalensis*

Family Varanidae

Suborder Sauria

Order Squamata

Size 6 ft (1.8 m) long

Key features Head relatively small and pointed; neck thick and muscular; limbs short; tail long and slightly compressed from side to side; dorsal pattern varies, but basic coloration is black, gray, or brown with lighter markings

Habits In wet habitats rests on submerged vegetation; in other places climbs trees or forages on the ground; takes refuge in tree hollows, burrows, or termite mounds during inactive periods

Breeding Mating, egg laying, and hatching vary from region to region; on average female lays 1–3 clutches of a maximum of 30 eggs that hatch after 170–250 days

Diet Insects, beetles, snails, small amphibians, small mammals, and lizards

Habitat Variable from rain forest to swamps to more arid, rocky regions as well as cultivated areas

Distribution Eastern Iran, Afghanistan, Pakistan, India, Nepal, Sri Lanka, Bangladesh, Myanmar, Malaysia, Sumatra, Java, and the Sunda Islands

Status Endangered (IUCN) in some parts of its range; listed in CITES Appendix I

Similar species None

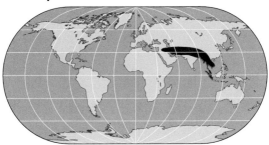

Sand Monitor

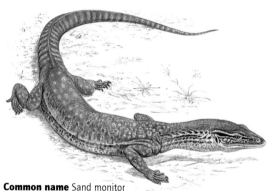

Common name Sand monitor
(Gould's monitor, "racehorse goanna")

Scientific name *Varanus gouldii*

Family Varanidae

Suborder Sauria

Order Squamata

Size From 4 ft (1.2 m) to 5.3 ft (1.6 m) long

Key features Body elongated but stout; head relatively small with pointed snout; tail rounded with dorsal crest on last part; front legs large and strong for digging; coloration variable depending on locality but usually tan to yellow with contrasting spots

Habits Terrestrial with a wide home range; spends much of the day foraging for food; rests in burrows during inactive periods

Breeding Average clutch size of 6-7 eggs laid in excavated nest in soil or in termite mounds; eggs hatch after about 3-4 months

Diet Lizards, small mammals, eggs, and birds

Habitat Subhumid to arid areas, deserts to jungle rivers; generally favors sandy soil; in the north of its range habitat includes tropical woodland

Distribution Most of mainland Australia (except the extreme south and Victoria); recently reported in New Guinea

Status Common

Similar species The Argus monitor, *V. panoptes*

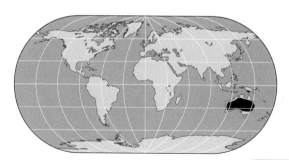

Komodo Dragon

Common name Komodo dragon

Scientific name *Varanus komodoensis*

Family Varanidae

Suborder Sauria

Order Squamata

Size Up to a maximum of 10.3 ft (3.1 m) long

Key features Body very large; head relatively small; ear openings visible; teeth sharp and serrated; tail powerful; strong limbs and claws for digging; scales small, uniform, and rough; color varies from brown to brownish or grayish red; juveniles are green with yellow-and-black bands

Habits Spends much of the time foraging for food; digs burrows to which it retreats at night and during hot weather

Breeding Female lays clutch of up to 30 eggs (depending on size of female); eggs buried in earth and hatch after 7.5–8 months

Diet Insects, reptiles, eggs, small mammals, deer, goats, wild boar, pigs

Habitat Lowland areas ranging from arid forest to savanna, including dry riverbeds

Distribution Islands of Komodo, Rinca, Padar, and Western Flores in Indonesia

Status Vulnerable (IUCN); listed in CITES Appendix I; protected locally

Similar species None

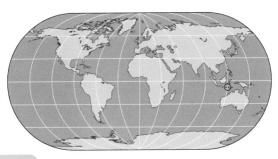

Nile Monitor

Common name
Nile monitor

Scientific name *Varanus niloticus*

Family Varanidae

Suborder Sauria

Order Squamata

Size Up to 6.5 ft (2 m) long

Key features Body elongated with muscular limbs and sharp claws; skin tough with small, beadlike scales; tail laterally compressed; basic coloration olive-green to black with variable lighter markings

Habits Spends nonhunting daylight hours basking on rocks and branches or in water; uses burrows and old termite mounds at night; can swim well

Breeding Female lays up to 60 eggs in a clutch, often in termite mounds; eggs hatch after 150–200 days

Diet Insects, eggs, birds, small mammals, crustaceans, amphibians, snakes, lizards

Habitat Grassland, fringes of deserts, rain forests, even cultivated areas—almost anywhere providing there is a permanent body of water

Distribution Eastern and southern Africa from Egypt to South Africa

Status Common

Similar species None

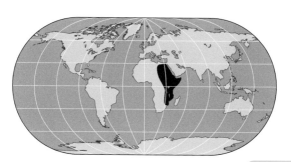

Borneo Earless Monitor

Common name Borneo earless monitor

Scientific name *Lanthanotus borneensis*

Family Lanthanotidae

Suborder Sauria

Order Squamata

Size From 17 in (43 cm) to 20 in (50 cm) long

Key features Nose blunt; tail as long as body; eyes small; no external ear openings; rows of dorsal scales are keeled and interspersed with smaller, granular scales

Habits Active at dusk and at night; spends much of the time either in burrows in riverbanks or in the water; semiaquatic and a burrower

Breeding Female lays 1 clutch of up to 6 eggs

Diet Thought to include worms, fish, and eggs

Habitat Riverbanks in rain forest and also shallow water in rice paddies

Distribution Sarawak and Borneo

Status Vulnerable (IUCN)

Similar species None

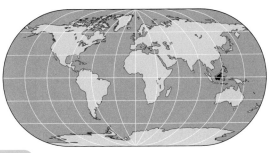

Sooty Worm Lizard

Common name Sooty worm lizard
(black-and-white worm lizard)

Scientific name *Amphisbaenia fuliginosa*

Family Amphisbaenidae

Suborder Amphisbaenia

Order Squamata

Size From 12 in (30 cm) to 18 in (46 cm) long

Key features Skull bony, covered with large plates; body
cylindrical with a shallow fold down either flank and
covered with rings of small, square scales (annuli); tail
short with a blunt end; one of the more distinctively
marked worm lizards with irregular black markings
on a white or pinkish background

Habits Burrower; rarely seen on the surface

Breeding Egg layer

Diet Invertebrates; occasionally small vertebrates

Habitat Rain forests, forest clearings

Distribution Northern South America from southern Panama to
Peru and Bolivia across to Brazil and north to Venezuela,
Guyana, Surinam, French Guyana, and the island of
Trinidad

Status Common in suitable habitat

Similar species None; the other large worm lizard in the
region is *A. alba*, which lacks the black markings;
distinguishable from snakes by the annular arrangement
of scales and the lack of functional eyes

Iberian Worm Lizard

Common name Iberian worm lizard (European worm lizard)

Scientific name *Blanus cinereus*

Family Amphisbaenidae

Suborder Amphisbaenia

Order Squamata

Size Maximum 12 in (30 cm) long but usually considerably smaller

Key features Resembles a purple or brown earthworm, but on close examination a mouth and vestigial eyes can be seen; head is distinct from the body, having an obvious fold of skin immediately behind it

Habits Subterranean burrower

Breeding Egg layer; clutch consists of a single egg

Diet Ants, grubs, and other small invertebrates

Habitat Varied (but avoids compacted soils)

Distribution Southern two-thirds of Spain and Portugal

Status Probably common in suitable habitats

Similar species None in the region; the Anatolian worm lizard, *B. strauchii*, is found on the islands and mainland of the eastern Mediterranean and into the Middle East; it lacks the prominent fold of skin behind the head

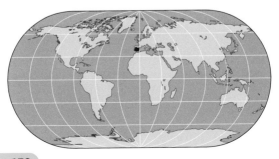

Ajolote

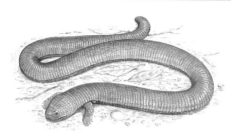

Common name Ajolote (mole lizard, Mexican worm lizard)

Scientific name *Bipes biporus*

Family Bipedidae

Suborder Amphisbaenia

Order Squamata

Size From 7 in (18 cm) to 9 in (23 cm) long

Key features Resembles a long earthworm with two front legs; legs are situated very far forward just behind the head and are thick and powerful like those of a mole; body has little or no pigment and is pinkish white; the vestigial eyes and the body rings show up well; a shallow groove runs along its flanks

Habits Subterranean, only rarely appearing on the surface

Breeding Egg layer; female lays 1–4 eggs in summer; eggs hatch after about 2 months

Diet Small invertebrates, especially termites and their larvae; also larger animals, such as small lizards

Habitat Dry, sandy plains, often with scattered bushes

Distribution Baja California, Mexico

Status Very common in suitable habitats

Similar species 2 other species of *Bipes* live in mainland Mexico

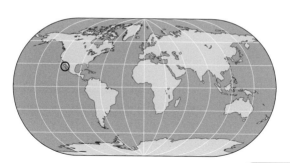

Texas Thread Snake

Common name Texas thread snake (plains slender blind snake)

Scientific name *Leptotyphlops dulcis*

Family Leptotyphlopidae

Suborder Serpentes

Order Squamata

Length About 12 in (30 cm)

Key features Pinkish with smooth, shiny scales; body very slender; tail bears inconspicuous horny spike; eyes are darker patches

Habits Burrower, rarely coming onto the surface and only at night

Breeding Egg layer, with clutches of up to 8 eggs

Diet Larvae and pupae of ants and termites, as well as other soft-bodied invertebrates

Habitat Prairies, lightly wooded places, and bare, rocky hillsides, but usually where there is some moisture in the soil

Distribution Southeastern United States west to Arizona and adjacent parts of northeastern Mexico

Status Common in suitable habitat, although rarely seen

Subspecies The plains thread snake, *L. d. dulcis;* the New Mexico thread snake, *L. d. dissectus*

Similar species Western thread snake, *L. humilis*

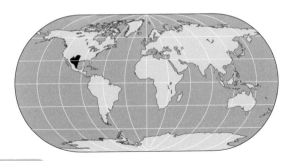

European Worm Snake

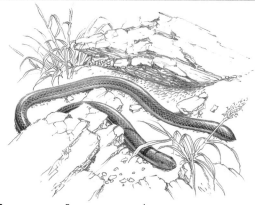

Common name European worm snake

Scientific name *Typhlops vermicularis*

Family Typhlopidae

Suborder Serpentes

Order Squamata

Length Up to 13 in (33 cm), but usually smaller

Key features Resembles a small, shiny worm, but with small eyes

Habits Burrower; often rests under half-buried stones; may be active on the surface at night

Breeding Lays about 6 eggs in an underground chamber; little known about incubation period or size and appearance of the young

Diet Ants and their larvae and other soft-bodied invertebrates

Habitat Dry, grassy, rocky hillsides, especially if there are patches of bare earth

Distribution Southeast Europe, Southwest Asia, and parts of the Middle East as far as Afghanistan

Status Common in suitable habitat, but often overlooked

Similar species None in the region, although similar species found in North Africa and farther east; could be confused with legless lizards from the region, but they are far more heavy bodied, have functional eyes, and are more alert and agile

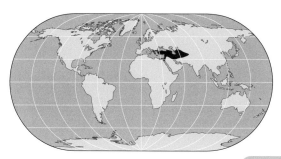

Red-Tailed Pipe Snake

Common name Red-tailed pipe snake (two-headed snake)

Scientific name *Cylindrophis ruffus*

Family Cylindrophiidae

Suborder Serpentes

Order Squamata

Length 27.5 in (70 cm)

Key features Body cylindrical with smooth scales; color dark purplish brown with narrow cream bars above and black and white below; underside of the tail is red

Habits Burrows in mud, damp soil, or leaf litter; active on the surface in the evening and at night

Breeding Gives birth to 5–10 live young

Diet Eels and snakes, often as long or longer than itself

Habitat Lowland forests, grasslands, and swamps up to 5,500 ft (1,700 m) elevation

Distribution Southeast Asia from southern China, Thailand, Laos, Vietnam, and Myanmar (Burma), through the Malaysian Peninsula to Borneo and parts of Indonesia

Status Common but rarely seen

Similar species Many small, dark-brown snakes in the region, but the red-tailed pipe snake is the only one with a red patch under its tail

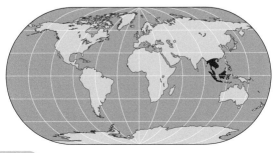

American Sunbeam Snake

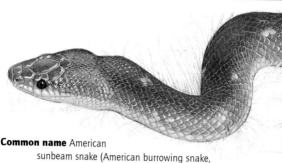

Common name American sunbeam snake (American burrowing snake, burrowing python)

Scientific name *Loxocemus bicolor*

Family Loxocemidae

Suborder Serpentes

Order Squamata

Length From 39 in (100 cm) to 4.3 ft (1.3 m)

Key features Body cylindrical with small, shiny scales; head barely wider than its neck; snout pointed; appears iridescent; dark gray or brown in color with strange, irregular white spots over body; some individuals have large white areas, giving them an almost piebald appearance; pelvic girdles present as well as vestigial hind limbs in the form of small spurs

Habits Probably a burrower but also active on the surface; nocturnal

Breeding Egg layer, with small clutches of 2–5 eggs; eggs hatch after about 65 days

Diet Other reptiles, including their eggs, and rodents

Habitat Tropical forests, including dry deciduous forests

Distribution Central America from western Mexico to Costa Rica

Status Common

Similar species None in the region; superficially similar to the Asian sunbeam snakes, *Xenopeltis* sp., with which it used to be classified

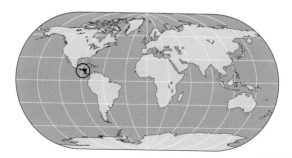

Arafura File Snake

Common name Arafura file snake

Scientific name *Acrochordus arafurae*

Family Acrochordidae

Suborder Serpentes

Order Squamata

Length 5 ft (1.5 m), but occasionally up to 8.1 ft (2.5 m)

Key features Appearance rather strange and unmistakable, with the skin appearing too big for the body; body has many small, granular, nonoverlapping scales that look and feel rough; color brown or gray on upper side with indistinct dark reticulations; head small with tiny eyes positioned on top; nostrils also on top with valves that allow the snake to close them; tongue longer than normal

Habits Entirely aquatic; may swim in open water but more commonly crawls over muddy bottoms

Breeding Live-bearer, with litters averaging about 17; may have long periods between breeding

Diet Fish

Habitat Mainly freshwater streams, rivers, and lagoons but also flooded land, swamps, estuaries

Distribution Northern Australia, southern New Guinea

Status Very common in suitable habitat

Similar species Two other file snakes are quite similar, but 1 species lives only in the sea and estuaries, and the other does not occur in the same area

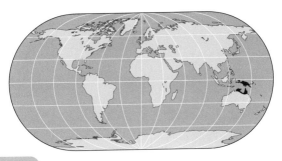

Common Boa

Common name Common boa (boa constrictor)

Scientific name *Boa constrictor*

Family Boidae

Suborder Serpentes

Order Squamata

Length Up to 13 ft (4 m) but often much smaller; island forms rarely more than 6.5 ft (2 m)

Key features Head wedge shaped; a dark line runs through each eye, widening toward the angle of the mouth; background color gray, brown, tan, or pink, with a series of large rounded saddles in maroon or dark brown down the back; tail saddles may be reddish

Habits Arboreal or terrestrial; often enters the water and is a good swimmer

Breeding Bears up to 60 live young but more commonly 10–15

Diet Small mammals; birds

Habitat Very adaptable; rain forests, deciduous forests, dry scrub, and even beaches; often common around human settlements

Distribution From northwestern Mexico through Central America and into South America as far as northern Argentina; also found on some West Indian islands (St. Lucia and Dominica)

Status Generally common, but some subspecies (e.g., Argentine boa, *B. c. occidentalis*) are Endangered (CITES Appendix I)

Similar species None

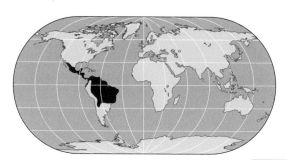

Dumeril's Boa

Common name Dumeril's boa

Scientific name *Boa dumerili* (formerly *Acrantophis dumerili*)

Family Boidae

Suborder Serpentes

Order Squamata

Length From 5 ft (1.5 m) to 6.5 ft (2 m)

Key features Body stocky with a narrow, elegant head; markings extremely intricate and include pale ovals along the middle of the back, surrounded by darker brown; some individuals have a pinkish or orange tinge, especially when young

Habits Forest dweller but rarely climbs, preferring to live on the forest floor, where it is well camouflaged

Breeding Live-bearer, with litters of 6–15, exceptionally as many as 20; young measure up to 18 in (45 cm) at birth

Diet Mainly mammals; occasionally birds

Habitat Dry forests

Distribution Madagascar, especially the south and southwest

Status Apparently common in areas where habitat has not been disturbed; habitat destruction for agriculture is a cause for concern; collecting for pet trade is controlled, and captive-bred animals are freely available

Similar species The Madagascan ground boa, *B. madagascariensis*, is slightly larger and darker in color; it has larger scales on its head than *B. dumerili* and is restricted to the damper eastern and northern regions of Madagascar

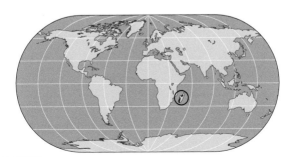

Emerald Tree Boa

Common name
Emerald tree boa

Scientific name *Corallus caninus*

Family Boidae

Suborder Serpentes

Order Squamata

Length From 5 ft (1.5 m) to 6.5 ft (2 m)

Key features Adults bright green with narrow white crossbars; sometimes yellow underneath; newborn young are bright yellow or red; scales covering the head are small and granular; lips bear prominent heat pits; eyes have vertical pupils

Habits Completely arboreal; rarely, if ever, comes down to the ground; when resting during the day, it drapes its coils over horizontal boughs in a characteristic way

Breeding Live-bearer, with up to 15 in a litter

Diet Birds and small mammals, which it catches at night

Habitat Lowland rain forests up to 3,000 ft (900 m)

Distribution South America (mainly within the Amazon Basin)

Status Common but hard to find; habitat destruction is its biggest threat

Similar species Green tree python, *Morelia viridis*, in Australasia; within its range it could possibly be confused with several green pit vipers

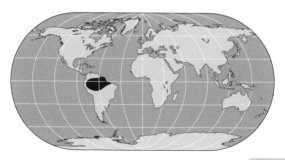

Pacific Ground Boa

Common name Pacific ground boa

Scientific name *Candoia carinata*

Family Boidae

Suborder Serpentes

Order Squamata

Length 24 in (60 cm) to 39 in (100 cm)

Key features Size, color, and markings very variable; head narrow and covered in small scales; snout sharply oblique when seen from the side; often has viperlike markings along the back; eyes small with vertical pupils; heat pits lacking

Habits Terrestrial or arboreal depending on location and presence of competing species

Breeding Live-bearer; litter size varies according to subspecies (*C. c. carinata* has about 6 large young, *C. c. paulsoni* has up to 50 very small young)

Diet Reptiles, amphibians, and small mammals

Habitat Rain forests and plantations

Distribution New Guinea, parts of Indonesia, and the Solomon Islands; also on many offshore islands

Status Locally common

Similar species New Guinea ground boa, or viper boa, *C. aspera*, which is shorter and stouter

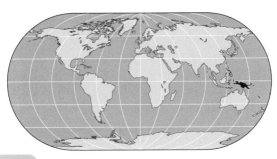

Rainbow Boa

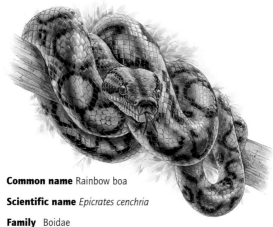

Common name Rainbow boa

Scientific name *Epicrates cenchria*

Family Boidae

Suborder Serpentes

Order Squamata

Length From 5 ft (1.5 m) to 6.5 ft (2 m)

Key features A powerful snake; body almost cylindrical with highly iridescent, glossy scales; markings varied according to 9 different subspecies

Habits Usually nocturnal; secretive and slow moving

Breeding Live-bearer; litters contain 10–30 young depending on subspecies—some have small litters of large young, others have large numbers of smaller young

Diet Mostly mammals

Habitat Rain forests, deciduous forests, open woodland, and pampas (grassland)

Distribution Central and South America from Panama to Argentina and Paraguay

Status Common

Similar species None, but variation in color and markings sometimes makes identification difficult

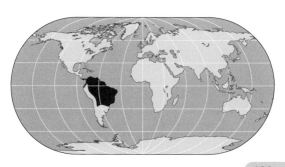

Anaconda

Common name Anaconda
(green anaconda)

Scientific name *Eunectes murinus*

Family Boidae

Suborder Serpentes

Order Squamata

Length Up to 33 ft (10 m) or more, but typically from 16.5 ft
(5 m) to 19.7 ft (6 m)

Key features Body massive; head narrow; neck short and thick;
head and body greenish in color; body has dark oval
spots along either side of the dorsal midline; a bold
black line runs diagonally back from each eye to the
angle of the jaw; eyes small and positioned near top of
head; nostrils also positioned on top of head; heat pits
absent; females more than twice the size of males

Habits Semiaquatic

Breeding Live-bearer with litters of up to 80, although litters of
10–20 are more usual

Diet Mammals, birds, and other reptiles

Habitat Swamps, slow-moving rivers, shallow lakes, lagoons, and
flooded grasslands

Distribution South America, mostly within the Amazon
and Orinoco Basins, but extending into coastal
southeastern Brazil

Status Common

Similar species Yellow anaconda, *E. notaeus*, is smaller with
overall yellow coloration; De Schauensee's anaconda,
E. deschauenseei, is similar to the yellow anaconda but
not always recognized as separate species; 2 subspecies,
E. m. murinus and *E. m. gigas*, differ mainly in head
coloration

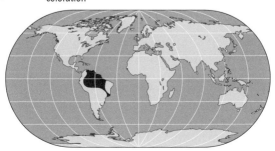

Rubber Boa

Common name
Rubber boa

Scientific name *Charina bottae*

Family Boidae

Suborder Serpentes

Order Squamata

Length Up to 31 in (79 cm); usually 12 in (30 cm)

Key features Looks and feels "rubbery"; brown, olive, or tan in color; body stocky and cylindrical; tail and head blunt in shape; top of head covered with large scales; eyes small; no heat pits; body scales are tiny, adding to the smooth, silky feel; small spurs on either side of cloaca, larger in males than in females

Habits Remains hidden during the day under bark or logs or in the burrows of small mammals; active at night even in quite low temperatures, when it hunts by poking around in crevices and entering rodent nests

Breeding Live-bearer with litters of 2–8 young

Diet Small mammals, birds (especially nestlings), salamanders, lizards, and snakes

Habitat Grassland, scrub, light woodland, and conifer forests in mountains

Distribution Western North America from British Columbia, Canada, to southern California and inland to central Wyoming; distribution patchy, only occurring where there is suitable habitat

Status Protected (CITES Appendix II) and nationally; probably not rare, but suffers from habitat destruction and collecting for the pet trade

Similar species None in the area; at least 3 subspecies recognized, but differences between them are slight, and they are not easily told apart

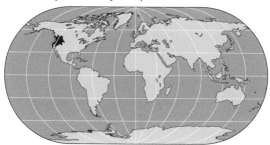

Rosy Boa

Common name Rosy boa

Scientific name *Charina trivirgata*

Family Boidae

Suborder Serpentes

Order Squamata

Length From 24 in (60 cm) to 39 in (100 cm)

Key features Body stout, with a thick neck so that the narrow head is not distinct from the body; head covered with many small scales; eyes small; no heat pits; various colors, usually arranged in 3 longitudinal stripes on a lighter background

Habits Active at night and in the evening; mainly terrestrial but climbs well among rocks

Breeding Live-bearer with litters of up to 12, although 4-6 is more typical

Diet Small mammals and birds

Habitat Rocky deserts and scrub, often along dried watercourses and near oases

Distribution Southwestern North America from southern California and Arizona throughout the length of the Baja California peninsula and into western Sonora (Mexico)

Status Common in suitable habitat; large numbers are killed on the road; also collected for the pet trade despite being protected (CITES Appendix II)

Similar species None in the region; the young of some forms could be mistaken for rubber boa, *C. bottae*, which favors a different habitat

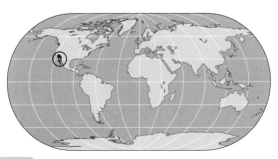

Children's Python

Common name
Children's python

Scientific name *Antaresia childreni*

Family Pythonidae

Suborder Serpentes

Order Squamata

Length Up to 39 in (100 cm), but typically about 30 in (75 cm)

Key features Smallish and slender with proportionately large eyes that are yellow in color; overall color light brown with numerous darker brown blotches on the back and sides; small heat pits located in the scales bordering the mouth

Habits Mostly ground dwelling; climbs well and is often found among rocks

Breeding Egg layer with clutches of about 6-12; female coils around eggs until they hatch

Diet Small mammals and birds; other reptiles

Habitat Very adaptable; rain forests, scrub, open woodlands, and deserts

Distribution Northern Australia from the Kimberley region to the Gulf of Carpentaria and western Queensland

Status Common

Similar species 3 other members of the genus *Antaresia* are quite similar

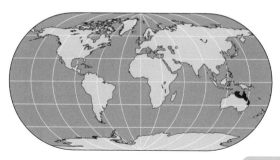

Black-Headed Python

Common name
Black-headed python

Scientific name *Aspidites melanocephalus*

Family Pythonidae

Suborder Serpentes

Order Squamata

Length Up to 10 ft (3 m), but normally about 5.5 ft (1.7 m)

Key features Body shape slender and graceful; head only slightly wider than the neck; snout blunt; head and the first few inches of the neck are deep glossy black; rest of body and tail are yellowish, gray, or more often reddish-brown with slightly darker irregular bars

Habits Spends much of its time underground, often in the burrows of small mammals or monitor lizards

Breeding Egg layer with clutches of 6–18 eggs (average 9); incubation period about 8 weeks

Diet Mostly reptiles, especially diurnal lizards and other snakes; also mammals and birds

Habitat Wooded grassland and open forests; may live in wet or dry places

Distribution Northern parts of Australia from the Kimberley region in the west to the east coast of Queensland

Status Fairly common in suitable habitat

Similar species The other member of the genus is the woma, *Aspidites ramsayi*, which lacks the black head and neck, but is otherwise similar; other black-headed snakes occur in Australia, but none grows as long or stocky as this one

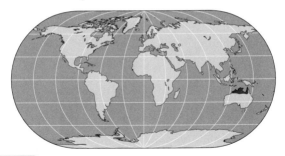

Amethystine Python

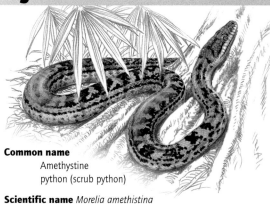

Common name
Amethystine
python (scrub python)

Scientific name *Morelia amethistina*

Family Pythonidae

Suborder Serpentes

Order Squamata

Length Variable; exceptionally large forms may grow to almost 28 ft (8.5 m)

Key features Body long and slender; head long, top is covered with a small number of large scales; heat pits on the lower labial scales and the first 2 or 3 pairs of upper labial scales; body scales smooth and iridescent; markings variable from place to place, may consist of dark-brown or black broken bars on a lighter-brown background

Habits Young are very agile and climb into trees and bushes; adults are more terrestrial

Breeding Egg layer with clutches of 6–18 eggs, the average being about 12

Diet Vertebrates of all kinds

Habitat Forests, including rain forests, coastal swamp forests, and open woodland; also secondary regrown forests, scrub, and plantations

Distribution New Guinea, parts of Indonesia, and extreme northern tip of Queensland, Australia

Status Common

Similar species Amethystine python may consist of 3 or more distinct species, varying in size, colors, markings, and geographical distribution

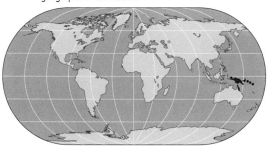

Carpet Python

Common name Carpet python, diamond python (depending on subspecies)

Scientific name *Morelia spilota*

Family Pythonidae

Suborder Serpentes

Order Squamata

Length Typically about 6.5 ft (2 m); occasionally up to 13 ft (4 m)

Key features Stocky body with a wide head distinct from its neck; top of head covered with small scales, but some of the centrally placed ones are larger; heat pits present in rostral scales and some upper and lower labial scales; markings extremely variable, but there is a tendency toward a pattern of dark bands on a lighter background; diamond python (*M. s. spilota*) is uniformly marked with black-edged yellow scales, with a vague pattern of lighter spots superimposed

Habits As varied as its appearance

Breeding Egg layer with clutches of up to 50 eggs brooded by the female; females breed every 2 to 3 years; eggs hatch after about 8 weeks

Diet A range of vertebrate prey depending on its age

Habitat Found in every conceivable habitat (forests, grasslands, deserts, urban, etc.) throughout its wide range

Distribution Throughout Australia (except for the arid interior and western parts) and New Guinea; also on several island groups

Status Common

Similar species Bredl's carpet python, *M. bredli*

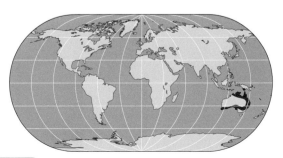

Green Tree Python

Common name Green tree python

Scientific name *Morelia viridis*
(formerly *Chondropython viridis*)

Family Pythonidae

Suborder Serpentes

Order Squamata

Length Average 5.2 ft (1.6 m) to 5.9 ft (1.8 m); maximum
7.2 ft (2.2 m)

Key features Adults bright green with white markings along
dorsal midline; juveniles yellow or orange; top of head
covered with many small scales; conspicuous heat pits in
the rostral scales, the first few upper labial scales, and in
most of the lower labial scales

Habits Tree dweller but may crawl on the ground at night in
search of new hunting possibilities; drapes coils over
horizontal branches

Breeding Egg layer with typical clutch of about 10 eggs; female
coils around the eggs and remains with them
throughout incubation period

Diet Adults feed on mammals and some birds; juveniles eat
lizards and possibly frogs

Habitat Forests; garden trees and hedges on the outskirts
of towns

Distribution New Guinea from sea level to 6,560 ft (2,000 m);
also found on many small islands off the mainland,
several Indonesian island groups, and at the very tip of
Cape York, Queensland, Australia

Status Common in suitable habitat

Similar species The emerald tree boa, *Corallus caninus* from
South America

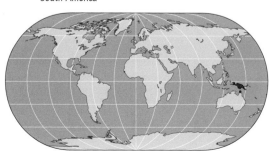

Burmese and Indian Pythons

Indian python (*Python molurus molurus*)

Common name Burmese python, Indian python (depending on subspecies), Indian rock python

Scientific name *Python molurus*

Family Pythonidae

Suborder Serpentes

Order Squamata

Length Maximum about 20 ft (over 6 m)

Key features Very heavy bodied; markings consist of a pattern of large, irregular, but interlocking blotches on a paler background; blotches dark brown on a lighter brown to tan background (Burmese python) or midbrown on a gray background (Indian python); dark arrowhead mark always present on top of head between the eyes; heat pits in rostral scales and some of the labial scales

Habits Live in dense forests and frequently climb into trees; elsewhere prefer riversides and often enter the water

Breeding Egg layers with large clutches of eggs brooded by the female

Diet Mammals up to the size of deer

Habitat Rain forests, clearings, plantations, and riversides

Distribution India, Sri Lanka (*P. m. molurus*); Myanmar (Burma), Thailand, South China, and Vietnam (*P. m. bivittatus*)

Status Common where suitable habitat remains but rare in places where the land has been extensively cleared; IUCN Endangered (Indian subspecies)

Similar species In places its range overlaps that of the reticulated python, *P. reticulatus*, but the 2 species are not easily confused

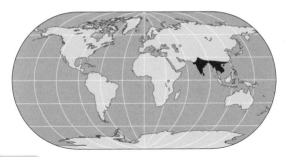

Royal Python

Common name Royal python
(ball python)

Scientific name *Python regius*

Family Pythonidae

Suborder Serpentes

Order Squamata

Length From 36 in (91 cm) to 5 ft (1.5 m)

Key features Small and thickset with a small head and short
tail; distinctive pattern of rounded brown or tan blotches
on a black background; usually a row of blotches down
the center of the back and a series of larger ones on its
flanks, sometimes with one or more dark spots in them

Habits Nocturnal; terrestrial, resting on the forest floor among
dead leaves or in burrows

Breeding Egg layer with small clutches of typically 3–6 large
eggs; incubation period about 8 weeks

Diet Small mammals

Habitat Lowland and coastal forests and adjoining grasslands

Distribution West and Central Africa

Status Becoming rare in places due to continued exploitation
for skins, meat, and the pet trade

Similar species None in the region; could possibly be confused
with the Angolan python, *P. anchietae*, which is a similar
shape, but lives farther south in southwestern Africa

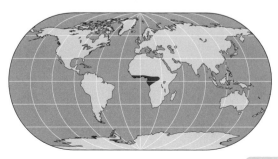

Reticulated Python

Common name Reticulated python

Scientific name *Python reticulatus*

Family Pythonidae

Suborder Serpentes

Order Squamata

Length Typically from about 15 ft (4.5 m) to 18 ft (5.5 m); possibly up to 33 ft (10 m), but many reports are exaggerated

Key features Often huge with a large, wide head; dark stripe runs along center of head; another stripe joins each eye to the angle of the jaw; eyes orange; deep heat pits on snout and in lip scales; head covered with large scales; patterning complex, with angular patches of olive or brown with narrow borders of black and yellow; also a series of white markings, often triangular, along the flanks

Habits Mainly nocturnal; lethargic, spending most of its time doing nothing

Breeding Egg layer with very large clutches of up to 100 eggs

Diet Medium and large mammals and birds

Habitat Varied; forests, riversides, fields, plantations, and even cities

Distribution Southeast Asia (Indochina through the Malaysian Peninsula, Indonesia, Borneo, and the Philippines)

Status Common, but habitat destruction and slaughter for the skin trade are reducing numbers alarmingly in places

Similar species None in the region

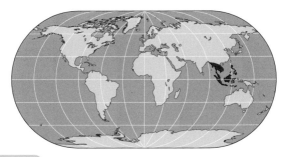

Long-Nosed Vine Snake

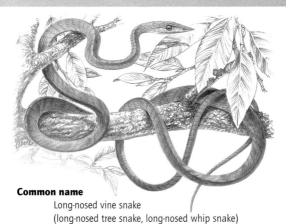

Common name
Long-nosed vine snake
(long-nosed tree snake, long-nosed whip snake)

Scientific name *Ahaetulla nasuta*

Subfamily Colubrinae

Family Colubridae

Suborder Serpentes

Order Squamata

Length 39 in (1 m) to 4 ft (1.2 m)

Key features Extremely slender snake; long tail; long pointed snout with grooves down either side; eyes large with horizontal pupils; usually green, but occasional specimens are brown or gray

Habits Arboreal, living in trees and shrubs; rarely comes down to the ground except to cross clearings (including roads)

Breeding Bears very small live young with litters of 20 or more

Diet Mainly lizards, although small birds and mammals taken occasionally

Habitat Forests and plantations

Distribution South and Southeast Asia from southeastern India through the Malay Peninsula and into Indochina

Status Common

Similar species Seven other species of *Ahaetulla* may look rather similar; two species of African twig snakes, *Thelotornis*, are the only other snakes with horizontal pupils

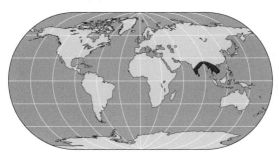

Asian Brown Tree Snake

Common name Asian brown tree snake (brown cat snake)

Scientific name *Boiga irregularis*

Subfamily Colubrinae

Family Colubridae

Suborder Serpentes

Order Squamata

Length From 6.5 ft (2 m) to 7.5 ft (2.3 m)

Key features Very long, slender snake; body compressed from side to side; usually brown but occasionally yellowish- or reddish-brown; may be traces of bars on its sides; eyes large with vertical pupils; scales down the middle of its back are larger than the other dorsal scales

Habits Arboreal, climbs in trees, shrubs, and buildings

Breeding Egg layer with clutches of about 6 eggs; hatching time unknown

Diet Anything, including birds, eggs, lizards, and small mammals

Habitat Lowland forests, plantations, and gardens

Distribution Southeast Asia, including parts of eastern Indonesia, New Guinea, the Solomon Islands, and northern Australia; introduced to the Pacific island of Guam

Status Abundant, especially on Guam, where it has no predators

Similar species There are a number of similar *Boiga* species, but *B. irregularis* is the most widespread and common

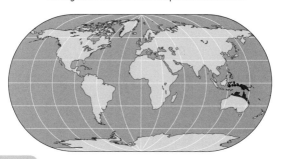

Western Shovel-Nosed Snake

Common name Western shovel-nosed snake

Scientific name *Chionactis occipitalis*

Subfamily Colubrinae

Family Colubridae

Suborder Serpentes

Order Squamata

Length 10 in (25 cm) to 17 in (43 cm)

Key features Small snake with shiny scales; pattern consists of black bars across a cream-colored background; snakes from some areas have secondary bars of red between the black ones; lower jaw deeply inset, and snout is flattened like a shovel

Habits Burrowing, active on the surface at night

Breeding Egg layer with 2–4 eggs laid in summer

Diet Invertebrates

Habitat Deserts

Distribution Southwestern North America

Status Common in suitable habitat

Similar species The Sonoran shovel-nosed snake, *C. palarostris*, has wider red bars, and the banded sand snake, *Chilomeniscus cinctus*, has a darker ground color and fewer rows of scales around its midbody; banded forms of the ground snake, *Sonora semiannulata*, lack the flattened head and shovel-shaped snout

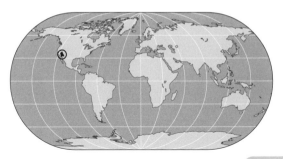

Western Whip Snake

Common name Western whip snake (dark-green snake)

Scientific name *Coluber viridiflavus*

Subfamily Colubrinae

Family Colubridae

Suborder Serpentes

Order Squamata

Length 5 ft (1.5 m), but occasionally longer

Key features Slender with a long tail; head small and elongated; eyes large with round pupils; scales smooth; occurs in 2 color forms—most have yellow backgrounds with extensive dark green or black markings, but some populations also include jet-black individuals

Habits Alert, fast-moving snake; hunts by day

Breeding Egg layer with clutches of 4–15 elongated eggs; eggs hatch after 40 to 56 days

Diet Mostly lizards, but adults also take small mammals, nestling birds, and other snakes

Habitat Dry places such as rocky hillsides, scrub, and field edges, especially near drystone walls

Distribution Europe (most of France except the north, northern Spain, Italy, parts of Switzerland and Croatia, and some Mediterranean islands, including Corsica and Sardinia)

Status Very common in suitable habitat

Similar species The Montpellier snake, *Malpolon monspessulanus*, in parts of southern France and the Balkan whip snake, *C. gemonensis*, in extreme northern Croatia

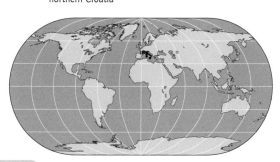

Common Egg-Eating Snake

Common name Common egg-eating snake (rhombic egg-eater)

Scientific name *Dasypeltis scabra*

Subfamily Colubrinae

Family Colubridae

Suborder Serpentes

Order Squamata

Length From 31 in (80 cm) to 39 in (1 m)

Key features Slender snake with a small head and rounded snout; markings often consist of darker blotches or chevrons on a light-gray, brown, or reddish background, but some individuals are plain colored; eyes small with vertical pupils; scales are very heavily keeled and have a rough texture

Habits Mostly terrestrial, although will climb into bushes and trees to find food; active at night

Breeding Egg layer with clutches of 6–18 eggs; may lay more than 1 clutch in a single breeding season; eggs hatch after about 60 days

Diet Birds' eggs

Habitat Lives in a variety of habitats and only avoids extreme deserts and rain forests

Distribution Africa south of the Sahara; also a small relict population in North Africa, in western Morocco

Status Very common but not often seen because of its nocturnal habits

Similar species Mimics a number of different venomous snakes (including adders, of which there are several species) according to its locality; there are 5 other species in the genus, some of which are similar to the common egg-eater

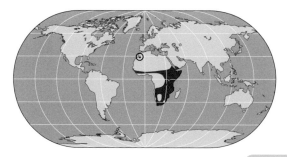

Boomslang

Common name
Boomslang

Scientific
name *Dispholidus typus*

Subfamily Colubrinae

Family Colubridae

Suborder Serpentes

Order Squamata

Length 5 ft (1.5 m) to 6.5 ft (2 m)

Key features Elongated body with a deep head and narrow neck; snout is pointed, and upper profile is steeply angled; eyes very large with round pupils; eyes of juveniles are bright emerald green in color; bodies of juveniles gray-brown, adults variously colored

Habits Arboreal

Breeding Egg layer with clutches of 10–14 eggs (occasionally more) laid in hollow tree trunks or leaf litter; eggs hatch after 60–90 days

Diet Lizards (especially chameleons) and birds; occasionally small mammals and frogs

Habitat Grassland with scattered trees and woods; also open woodland

Distribution Africa south of the Sahara, missing only from montane grasslands, deserts, and closed forests

Status Common

Similar species Two other genera of African tree snakes, *Thrasops* and *Rhamnophis*, are similar in size and coloration, and also have large eyes; none of them is dangerous to humans, however, although they have enlarged rear fangs and may bite

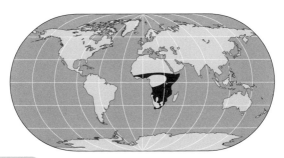

American Ratsnake

Black ratsnake
(*Elaphe obsoleta
obsoleta*)

Common name American ratsnake (black, Everglades, gray, Texas, or yellow ratsnake)

Scientific name *Elaphe obsoleta*

Subfamily Colubrinae

Family Colubridae

Suborder Serpentes

Order Squamata

Length From 39 in (1 m) to 8.1 ft (2.5 m)

Key features Long, muscular body; color varies depending on subspecies; juveniles marked differently than adults except in the gray ratsnake; scales weakly keeled on the back but smooth on the sides; distinct ridge along either side of the belly, which helps them climb

Habits Terrestrial and arboreal; black ratsnake swims well

Breeding Egg layer with clutches of 10–20 eggs, exceptionally up to 40 or more; eggs hatch after about 70 days

Diet Small mammals and birds

Habitat Varied but usually in places with trees; forest edges, thinly wooded hillsides, and hammocks

Distribution Throughout the eastern half of the United States

Status Common

Similar species Black form, *E. o. obsoleta*, may be mistaken for the black racer, *Coluber constrictor*, but that species has smooth scales and is fast moving

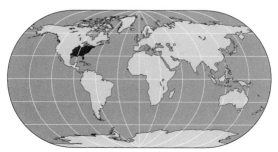

Leopard Snake

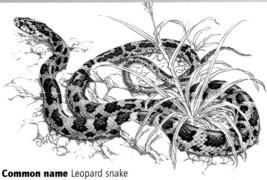

Common name Leopard snake

Scientific name *Elaphe situla*

Subfamily Colubrinae

Family Colubridae

Suborder Serpentes

Order Squamata

Length From 30 in (76 cm) to 36 in (91 cm)

Key features Body slender; head narrow; scales smooth; background color yellowish or buff; a row of red (sometimes brown) blotches runs down its back with a row of smaller spots on the flanks; each spot is edged in black; in some parts of the range the blotches may be divided into 2 parallel rows of smaller spots, or the markings may consist of 2 black-edged red stripes down the back

Habits Mainly ground dwelling, but it may climb into dry walls or scree

Breeding Egg layer with clutches of 2–8 eggs; eggs hatch after about 60 days

Diet Small rodents; occasionally lizards

Habitat Dry rocky places such as scrub-covered hillsides, scrub, and fields

Distribution Southeastern Europe, extending into western Asia (Turkey and the Crimean Peninsula)

Status Common in suitable habitat

Similar species None in the area; rare individuals with brown blotches could be confused with young four-lined snakes, *E. quatuorlineata*, or the transcaucasian ratsnake, *E. hohenackeri*, with whose range it overlaps in Turkey

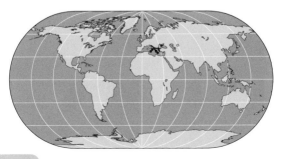

Corn Snake

Common name Corn snake (red ratsnake)

Scientific name *Elaphe guttata*

Subfamily Colubrinae

Family Colubridae

Suborder Serpentes

Order Squamata

Length From 43 in (110 cm) to 5.8 ft (1.8 m)

Key features Slender but muscular snake; head narrow; scales weakly keeled; eyes moderately large; pupils round; pattern consists of black-edged, deep-red to orange saddles on a background of gray, silver, or yellow; there is nearly always an arrow-shaped marking between the eyes; underneath it is black and white, often arranged in a checkered pattern

Habits Basically terrestrial but climbs well and may also spend time below ground

Breeding Egg layer with clutches of 5–25 eggs; eggs hatch after about 65 days

Diet Mostly small mammals (including bats) and occasional birds, but sometimes takes frogs and lizards when young

Habitat Open woods, hillsides, clearings in forests, and forest edges; often attracted to human settlements, especially farm buildings

Distribution Eastern United States to southern and northern Mexico

Status Common

Similar species Some milksnakes, such as the eastern milksnake, *Lampropeltis triangulum triangulum*, are similar but have smooth scales; young ratsnakes, *E. obsoleta*, are blotched but lack the arrowhead mark

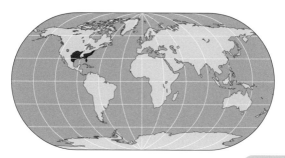

SNAKES

Common King Snake

Common name Common king snake (each subspecies has its own name, such as California king snake, black king snake, etc.)

Scientific name *Lampropeltis getula*

Subfamily Colubrinae

Family Colubridae

Suborder Serpentes

Order Squamata

Length 35 in (90 cm) to 5.8 ft (1.8 m)

Key features Muscular snake with an almost cylindrical body; small head hardly wider than neck; pupils round; smooth, glossy scales; markings variable but nearly always consist of a contrasting pattern of black (or dark brown) and white (or cream) in various arrangements; the Mexican subspecies is uniformly black

Habits Nocturnal; mainly terrestrial

Breeding Egg layer with clutches of up to 24 (but typically 6-12); eggs hatch after about 70 days

Diet Small mammals, lizards, and other snakes

Habitat Varied from lowland swamps to deserts

Distribution Southern half of the U.S. and adjacent parts of northern Mexico

Status Common in places

Similar species None in the area

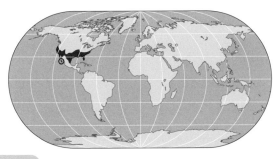

Milksnake

Red milksnake
(*Lampropeltis
triangulum syspila*)

Common name Milksnake (different
subspecies have different common names)

Scientific name *Lampropeltis triangulum*

Subfamily Colubrinae

Family Colubridae

Suborder Serpentes

Order Squamata

Length From 20 in (50 cm) to 6.5 ft (2 m)

Key features Cylindrical snake with glossy scales; head quite
small with no distinct neck; eyes also small and pupils
round; body usually marked with a combination of red,
black, and white (or yellow) bands, but some forms are
brown and gray, while others become uniform black
as adults

Habits Mostly nocturnal, sometimes active in the late evening
and early morning depending on locality; secretive

Breeding Egg layer with clutches of 4–15 eggs; eggs hatch after
40 to 60 days

Diet Small mammals, lizards, and other snakes

Habitat Extremely varied; found in almost every habitat within
its wide range except the most arid deserts

Distribution From Canada in the north through Central America
and south to Ecuador

Status Common in most places

Similar species At least 3 other members of the genus
Lampropeltis with red, black, and white bands (triads)
around their bodies, but they tend to be restricted to
montane habitats

Rough Green Snake

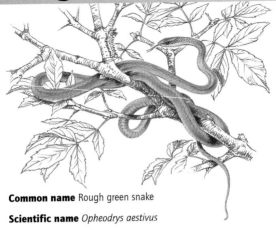

Common name Rough green snake

Scientific name *Opheodrys aestivus*

Subfamily Colubrinae

Family Colubridae

Suborder Serpentes

Order Squamata

Length From 22 in (56 cm) to 32 in (81 cm)

Key features Slender snake with an elongated head; scales keeled; color uniform light green; when dead, it quickly turns blue-gray; juveniles are also grayish-green

Habits Arboreal, lives among the leaves of trees and bushes; rarely descends to the ground except when moving to its egg-laying sites

Breeding Egg layer with clutches averaging 6 eggs; eggs hatch after 30–90 days

Diet Insects, mainly caterpillars, crickets, and grasshoppers

Habitat Dense stands of trees and shrubs, often those overhanging streams or the edges of lakes

Distribution North America; most of the eastern half of the United States, extending over the border into northeastern Mexico

Status Very common in suitable habitats

Similar species The smooth green snake, *Liochlorophis vernalis*, is similar but smaller with smooth scales

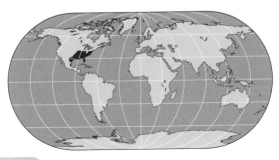

Ground Snake

Common name Ground snake (Prairie ground snake, Sonoran ground snake)

Scientific name *Sonora semiannulata*

Subfamily Colubrinae

Family Colubridae

Suborder Serpentes

Order Squamata

Length From 8 in (20 cm) to 19 in (48 cm)

Key features Small, slender snake with a narrow head no wider than its neck; eyes small; scales smooth; colors and markings highly variable

Habits Secretive; nocturnal and rarely seen

Breeding Egg layer with clutches of 4–6 eggs laid from June to August; eggs hatch after 50–70 days

Diet Invertebrates, especially spiders, scorpions, centipedes, crickets, and insect larvae

Habitat Dry places, including gravelly or sandy hollows and hillsides, preferring places where some loose material has collected

Distribution North America from southern Idaho to the tip of Baja California, Mexico, and from eastern California to central Texas, north to southern Kansas and Missouri

Status Common, although becoming rare in some places due to habitat destruction

Similar species The various color forms all seem to have lookalike species, including the young of venomous coral snakes

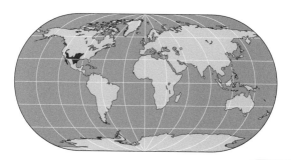

Tentacled Snake

Common name Tentacled snake

Scientific name *Erpeton tentaculatum*

Subfamily Homalopsinae

Family Colubridae

Suborder Serpentes

Order Squamata

Length From 24 in (60 cm) to 35 in (90 cm)

Key features Stout, almost rectangular in cross-section; head barely wider than neck; a pair of short fleshy "tentacles" on its snout; dorsal scales heavily keeled; ventral scales greatly reduced in size and form a narrow ridge along the snake's central midline; brown in color with darker longitudinal stripes along its length

Habits Totally aquatic; it apparently never leaves the water voluntarily and is practically helpless on land; if its pond dries out, it burrows into the mud

Breeding Live-bearer with litters of 5–15

Diet Fish and aquatic invertebrates

Habitat Ponds, slow-moving rivers, and swamps

Distribution Southeast Asia

Status Common; may occur at high densities in suitable habitats

Similar species None

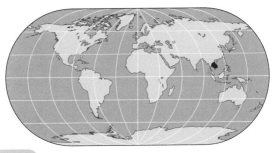

Brown House Snake

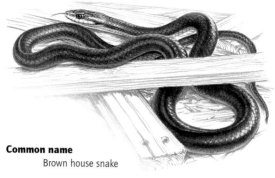

Common name
Brown house snake

Scientific name *Lamprophis fuliginosus*

Subfamily Boodontinae

Family Colubridae

Suborder Serpentes

Order Squamata

Length 35 in (90 cm) to 4.9 ft (1.5 m)

Key features Body slender but muscular with smooth scales; narrow head only slightly wider than neck; eyes small with vertical pupils; color varies from pale orange-brown through warm medium brown to dark olive or black; 4 cream lines on the head—1 pair of lines runs from the snout through the eye and stops on the neck, another is lower down, running along the edge of the upper jaw; underside is pearly white and highly iridescent

Habits Nocturnal; terrestrial

Breeding Female lays clutches of 5–16 eggs; eggs hatch after 60–90 days

Diet Mainly rodents, but birds, lizards, and frogs are sometimes eaten

Habitat Open grassland, arid rocky scrubland, cultivated ground, and around human dwellings

Distribution Most of Africa south of the Sahara; also found in a small area of North Africa in western Morocco

Status Common

Similar species Other house snakes can be confused with this species; youngsters are sometimes mistaken for venomous species such as cobras and mambas; but the cream lines on its head are characteristic

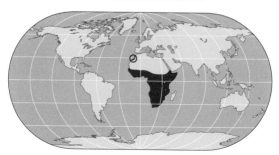

Leaf-Nosed Vine Snake

Common name Leaf-nosed vine snake

Scientific name *Langaha madagascariensis*

Subfamily Boodontinae

Family Colubridae

Suborder Serpentes

Order Squamata

Length 28 in (71 cm) to 35 in (89 cm)

Key features Body very slender; scales heavily keeled; tail long; eyes have vertical pupils; most remarkable characteristic is the extension to the tip of the snout; color brown, but males and females differ in their markings

Habits Arboreal and diurnal

Breeding Egg layer; small clutches of typically 3 eggs; eggs hatch after about 64–67 days

Diet Lizards; possibly other small vertebrates

Habitat Forests

Distribution Madagascar

Status Uncommon

Similar species 2 other members of the genus: the southern leaf-nosed vine snake, *L. alluaudi*, and the northern leaf-nosed vine snake, *L. pseudoalluaudi*; otherwise, it is impossible to confuse it with any other snake

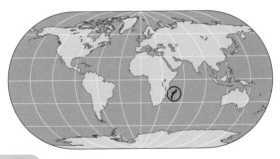

Grass Snake

Common name
    Grass snake (ringed snake, collared snake)

Scientific name *Natrix natrix*

Subfamily Natricinae

Family Colubridae

Suborder Serpentes

Order Squamata

Length 47 in (1.2 m) to 6.6 ft (2 m)

Key features Slender when young (females become more stocky as they grow); head well separated from neck; eyes moderately large with round pupils; scales keeled; body usually olive-brown or olive-green with a yellow or white crescent bordered by black behind the head; upper lips also yellowish and marked with a number of black bars; in some places grass snakes can be entirely black, black with white specks, or checkered black and gray

Habits Semiaquatic, swimming on the surface and diving occasionally

Breeding Egg layer with typical clutches of 8–40 eggs; eggs hatch after 42–70 days

Diet Frogs, toads, newts, and fish

Habitat Usually found around fresh water, including ponds, lakes, canals, and slow-moving rivers

Distribution Most of Europe, parts of North Africa and the Middle East, and a large part of Central Asia

Status Common but becoming less so in heavily populated areas

Similar species Two European members of the genus are similar but smaller. An Asian species, *N. megalocephala*, has a slightly larger head. Young Aesculapian snakes, *Elaphe longissima*, also have yellow patches behind the head

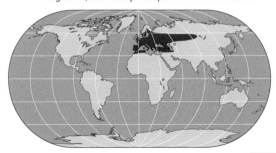

Southern Water Snake

Banded water snake
*(Nerodia fasciata
fasciata)*

Common name Southern water snake

Scientific name *Nerodia fasciata*

Subfamily Natricinae

Family Colubridae

Suborder Serpentes

Order Squamata

Length 39 in (1 m) to 5.25 ft (1.6 m)

Key features Body thick; head broad; snout oval; eyes large with round pupils; scales heavily keeled; usually brown with darker crossbands but may also be red, orange, or olive-green; in the wild often caked with mud, and markings can be hard to define; large individuals, especially females, sometimes become totally black

Habits Semiaquatic; can be bad tempered and hiss, strike, and bite, but usually less aggressive than other water snakes

Breeding Live-bearer with litters of up to 50; gestation period about 70–80 days

Diet Fish and amphibians

Habitat Freshwater ponds, lakes, and swamps; sometimes in brackish waters near the coast (e.g.,the Mississippi Delta); related species also occur in brackish and salt water along the Gulf Coast of Texas

Distribution Southeastern North America

Status Very common

Similar species Other water snakes are found in the region, but the species most likely to cause confusion is the venomous cottonmouth, *Agkistrodon piscivorus*

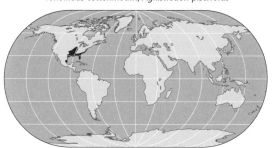

Common Garter Snake

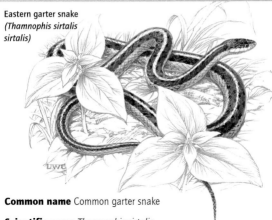

Eastern garter snake
*(Thamnophis sirtalis
sirtalis)*

Common name Common garter snake

Scientific name *Thamnophis sirtalis*

Subfamily Natricinae

Family Colubridae

Suborder Serpentes

Order Squamata

Length From 18 in (45 cm) to 4.25 ft (1.3 m)

Key features Body slender; head well separated from neck; large eyes with round pupils; keeled scales; pattern consists of several longitudinal stripes from neck to tail, but width and color of stripes depend on locality

Habits Semiaquatic in most places; diurnal and very alert

Breeding Live-bearer, with litters of up to 24; gestation period 60–90 days

Diet Amphibians, fish, and invertebrates such as worms

Habitat Ditches, ponds, streams, damp meadows, marshes, parks, and gardens; from sea level to 8,000 ft (2,450 m)

Distribution North America (Atlantic to Pacific coasts and Canada to the Southwest and Southeast); absent from deserts

Status Common in most places, but some forms are rare: The San Francisco garter snake, *T. s. tetrataenia*, is one of North America's rarest snakes

Similar species Garter snakes in general can be difficult to identify since most of them are striped

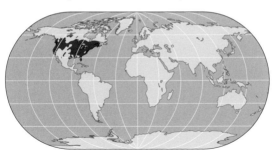

Asian Slug Snakes

Common name Asian slug snakes
(Asian snail-eating snakes)

Scientific name *Pareas* sp.

Subfamily Pareatinae

Family Colubridae

Suborder Serpentes

Order Squamata

Length 12 in (30 cm) to 30 in (76 cm)

Key features Long and slender or more robust depending on habits; most have a broad head, narrow neck, and large eyes; range of colors and markings, but most are some shade of brown or gray with small, indistinct dorsal spots and bars

Habits Strictly nocturnal; some species climb, and others live on the ground

Breeding Females lay small clutches of 2–4 eggs

Diet Slugs and snails; possibly other soft-bodied invertebrates

Habitat Varied, including rain forests, montane forests, plantations, and gardens

Distribution Southeast Asia

Status Some are common, but others are rare and poorly known

Similar species Many other small Asian snakes can look similar, but the scale arrangement on their chin makes them readily identifiable

White-spotted slug snake *(Pareas margaritophorus)*

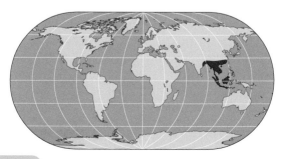

Ringneck Snake

Common name Ringneck snake

Scientific name *Diadophis punctatus*

Subfamily Uncertain, possibly Xenodontinae

Family Colubridae

Suborder Serpentes

Order Squamata

Length From 8 in (20 cm) to 30 in (76 cm)

Key features Body black, blue-black, dark- or olive-brown with a red or yellow underside and a collar of similar color just behind the head; scales smooth; head is small and hardly distinct from the neck; eyes also small

Habits Secretive, hides during the day; active at night or after rain in the early morning and evening

Breeding Egg layer with clutches of 2–10 eggs (usually 2–6) in June or July; eggs hatch after 28–42 days

Diet Invertebrates such as earthworms, small amphibians, lizards, and snakes

Habitat Damp places such as wood and forest edges, fields, farms, and gardens; in drier regions restricted to the areas around ponds and watercourses

Distribution Much of North America from coast to coast, including southern parts of Canada, extending to northern and north-central Mexico; possibly introduced to the Cayman Islands, West Indies

Status Very common to rare depending on locality

Similar species In Florida the red-bellied swamp snake, *Seminatrix pygaea*, or the worm snake, *Carphophis amoenus*, but they lack the red or yellow collar

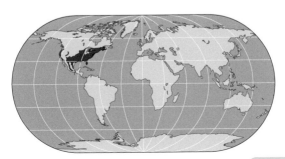

Western Hognose Snake

Common name Western hognose snake (puff adder—a ocal name, not to be confused with the venomous African viper of the same name)

Scientific name *Heterodon nasicus*

Subfamily Xenodontinae

Family Colubridae

Suborder Serpentes

Order Squamata

Length 16 in (40 cm) to 35 in (90 cm)

Key features Pointed, upturned snout; stout body and thick neck with heavily keeled scales; usually brown but can be yellowish with well-defined blotches down its back

Habits Diurnal; terrestrial and semiburrowing

Breeding Female lays clutches of 4–23 eggs that hatch after 50–62 days

Diet Toads, frogs, lizards, snakes, reptile eggs, small rodents, and birds

Habitat Well-drained shortgrass prairie, rocky semidesert, fields and wood edges, chaparral, and deserts; also found around human dwellings

Distribution North America (central states) extending into southern Canada and northern Mexico

Status Common and widespread but becoming scarce due to habitat destruction in places

Similar species Eastern hognose snake, *H. platyrhinos*, but its snout is less upturned, and body blotches are squarer

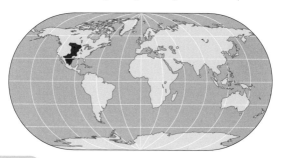

Centipede-Eating Snakes

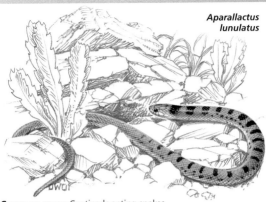

Aparallactus lunulatus

Common name Centipede-eating snakes

Scientific name *Aparallactus* sp.

Subfamily Aparallactinae

Family Atractaspididae

Suborder Serpentes

Order Squamata

Length 8 in (20 cm) to 18 in (45 cm)

Key features Small, thin snakes; heads small; eyes tiny with round pupils; bodies typical of burrowing snakes—cylindrical in shape with short tails and shiny scales; mostly brown in color with black "caps" on top of their heads

Habits Burrowing in loose soil under rocks or logs; may emerge onto the surface at night, especially after rain

Breeding 10 species are egg layers generally with clutches of 2–4 eggs, but *A. jacksoni* bears live young

Diet Centipedes, except *A. modestus*, which eats earthworms

Habitat Grassland with sandy soil; forests

Distribution Africa south of the Sahara

Status Probably common, although rarely seen; 1 species, the Mozambique centipede-eater, *A. nigriceps*, may be endangered

Similar species Their small size and slender bodies set them apart from most other snakes, but there are similar species throughout the region

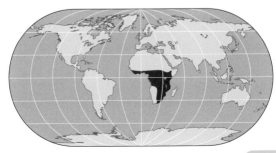

Mambas

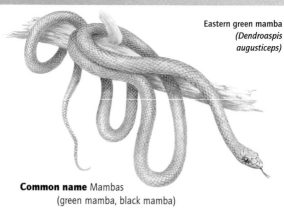

Eastern green mamba
(*Dendroaspis
augusticeps*)

Common name Mambas
(green mamba, black mamba)

Scientific name *Dendroaspis* sp.

Subfamily Elapinae

Family Elapidae

Suborder Serpentes

Order Squamata

Length From 5 ft (1.5 m) to 14 ft (4.3 m)

Key features Body long and slender with smooth scales; head
elongated; 3 species are green; the 4th is gray or brown;
mambas are never black, except for interior of the mouth

Habits The 3 green species are tree dwelling; the black mamba
lives on the ground among rocks or in low bushes and
trees; active by day; very alert and very fast moving

Breeding All are egg layers, laying clutches of 6–17 eggs; eggs
hatch after about 80 days

Diet Rodents, bats, birds, and their young

Habitat Forests (3 green species); savanna (black mamba)

Distribution Sub-Saharan Africa from the west across to the
Indian Ocean coast and south to eastern South Africa

Status Numerous in places, although forest species have
suffered through habitat destruction; none are as
common as in former times

Similar species Large adult black mambas are unmistakable,
but juveniles of all species can be confused with many
similar others

Venom Very potent; bites are often fatal, especially those of the
black mamba

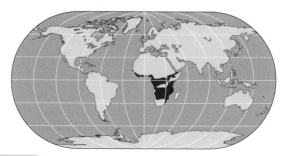

American Coral Snakes

Sonoran coral snake
(Micruroides euryxanthus)

Common name
American coral snakes

Scientific name *Micrurus* sp. and *Micruroides euryxanthus*

Subfamily Elapinae

Family Elapidae

Suborder Serpentes

Order Squamata

Length From 10.5 in (27 cm) to 5 ft (1.5 m)

Key features Cylindrical snakes; usually slender, but a few species are stocky; head small and a little wider than the neck; tail short; eyes small and black; scales smooth and shiny; typically brightly colored in rings of red, black, and yellow (or white), but there is some variation

Habits Mostly burrowing and secretive, although they can be seen on the surface at least occasionally; 1 species is semiaquatic

Breeding Egg layers, but details of breeding behavior are lacking for most species

Diet Snakes, burrowing lizards, and worm lizards; *Micrurus surinamensis* eats eels

Habitat Varied; from deserts to rain forests

Distribution North America (2 species) through Central America (many species) and into South America as far south as central Argentina

Status Common in places, but some species are known from only a few specimens

Similar species Many, all of which may be mimics

Venom Dangerously neurotoxic; bites may be life threatening unless treated

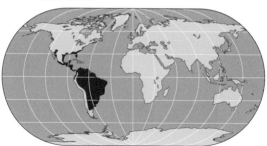

Indian Cobra

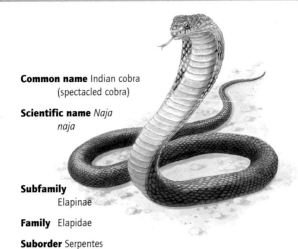

Common name Indian cobra (spectacled cobra)

Scientific name *Naja naja*

Subfamily Elapinae

Family Elapidae

Suborder Serpentes

Order Squamata

Length From 4 ft (1.2 m) to 5.5 ft (1.7 m)

Key features Body cylindrical with smooth scales and large shields on the head; usually brown, sometimes black, with a white or cream "spectacle" marking on the back of its neck only visible when it spreads its hood

Habits Usually day-active but also active in the evening, especially in places where there is human activity

Breeding Egg layer with clutches of 12–22 eggs; larger clutches are known but are unusual; eggs hatch after about 8–12 weeks

Diet Frogs, toads, snakes, mice, rats, and birds; appears to have no preference

Habitat A generalist living in forests, open grasslands, fields, and gardens; often attracted to human settlements

Distribution Indian subcontinent from the southern Himalayas to Sri Lanka

Status Becoming rare in places; in India considered endangered locally

Similar species Other cobras in neighboring regions

Venom Very potent; easily capable of killing an adult human

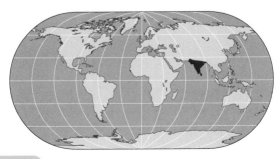

Cape Cobra

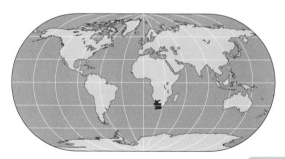

Common name Cape cobra

Scientific name *Naja nivea*

Subfamily Elapinae

Family Elapidae

Suborder Serpentes

Order Squamata

Length From 4 ft (1.2 m) to 5.5 ft (1.7 m); in exceptional cases up to 6.6 ft (2 m)

Key features Body slender, backbone slightly prominent; tail long; head roughly triangular, swelling noticeably behind the eyes to accommodate large venom glands; snout blunt; scales smooth and glossy; color variable, typically pale yellow but also reddish, brown, olive, or black; coloration can be uniform or with lighter or darker spots and speckles

Habits Alert, quick moving; active in the day

Breeding Egg layer; eggs laid in clutches of 8–20 in rodent burrows, termite mounds, or other underground cavities; eggs hatch after about 8 weeks

Diet Mainly mice and rats; also frogs, toads, lizards, snakes, and birds

Habitat Dry, sandy areas; mainly inland but also in coastal scrub and on mountainsides up to 8,000 ft (2,400 m)

Distribution South Africa, Namibia, and Botswana

Status Common

Similar species The black form is easily confused with the black spitting cobra, *Naja nigricollis woodi*, and with the black form of the mole snake, *Pseudaspis cana*

Venom Extremely potent, far more so than that of any other African cobra

King Cobra

Common name King cobra (hamadryad)

Scientific name *Ophiophagus hannah*

Subfamily Elapinae

Family Elapidae

Suborder Serpentes

Order Squamata

Length Usually from 10 ft (3 m) to 16.6 ft (5 m) but can reach 18 ft (5.5 m)

Key features Large but fairly nondescript; body slender with smooth scales; yellowish- or greenish- brown in color; juveniles are more brightly colored, being dark with narrow yellow or cream chevrons across the back and a boldly barred head; spreads a long, narrow hood when aroused

Habits Active on the ground during the day or night

Breeding Egg layer with clutches of 20–50 eggs; eggs hatch after about 60–70 days

Diet Other snakes; sometimes lizards

Habitat Primary forests

Distribution Eastern India, Indochina, and Southeast Asia

Status Locally common, but in a diminishing number of places

Similar species The Indian ratsnake, *Ptyas mucosus* (although it does not spread a hood); other hooded snakes in the region are all *Naja* species cobras (considerably smaller and with wider hoods)

Venom Highly venomous; life threatening within minutes, but bites are rare

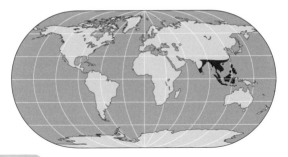

Taipans

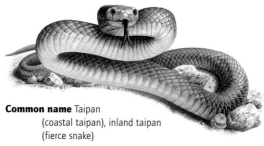

Common name Taipan
(coastal taipan), inland taipan
(fierce snake)

Scientific name *Oxyuranus scutellatus* (coastal taipan) and
O. microlepidotus (inland taipan)

Subfamily Hydrophiinae

Family Elapidae

Suborder Serpentes

Order Squamata

Length From 6.5 ft (2 m) to 12 ft (3.6 m)

Key features Body large and cylindrical; head narrow with
vertical sides; usually some shade of brown; coastal
taipan sometimes has a pale head, inland taipan may
have a black head and neck; coastal taipans from New
Guinea may be brown with a wide rust-colored stripe
down the back, or they may be uniform black

Habits Terrestrial; diurnal; fast and alert

Breeding Egg layers with clutches of up to 22 eggs; eggs hatch
after about 9–10 weeks

Diet Mammals

Habitat Forests, wooded grassland (coastal taipan); dry flood
plains (inland taipan)

Distribution Northern Australia and southern New Guinea
(coastal taipan); east-central Australia (inland taipan)

Status Common in places but shy and rarely seen

Similar species Adults distinctive because of their size; juveniles
can be confused with other species, such as the eastern
brown snake, *Pseudonaja textilis*, which is also
dangerous

Venom Both have exceedingly powerful venom; that of the
inland taipan is most destructive and is considered
to be the most potent of any terrestrial snake

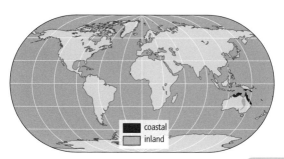

coastal
inland

Australian Tiger Snakes

Notechis scutatus

Common name
Australian tiger snake, common tiger snake, mainland tiger snake, black tiger snake

Scientific name *Notechis scutatus* (mainland tiger snake) and *N. ater (*black tiger snake)

Subfamily Hydrophiinae

Family Elapidae

Suborder Serpentes

Order Squamata

Length From 4 ft (1.2 m) to 7 ft (2.1 m)

Key features Body stout with large satiny scales; head large; snout blunt; eyes small; may flatten its neck when annoyed does not rear up and spread a hood; body dull black or dark brown with a yellow underside; distinctive yellow bands extend from beneath onto the flanks, becoming narrower toward the midline; the black tiger snake is almost always completely black

Habits Diurnal; terrestrial

Breeding Live-bearers with large litters usually of 10–40

Diet Frogs, lizards, birds, and small mammals

Habitat Varied: rain forest, grassland, swamps, and around farms

Distribution Southeastern and southwestern Australia (*N. scutatus*), Tasmania, and a small part of South Australia, including Flinders Range, Eyre Peninsula, Yorke Peninsula, and Kangaroo Island (*N. ater*)

Status Common

Similar species None in the region

Venom Very potent

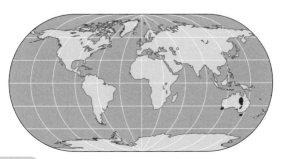

Yellow-Lipped Sea Krait

Common name Yellow-lipped sea krait

Scientific name *Laticauda colubrina*

Subfamily Hydrophiinae

Family Elapidae

Suborder Serpentes

Order Squamata

Length From 36 in (91 cm) to 6.6 ft (2 m)

Key features Body muscular and cylindrical except for the tail, which is flattened from side to side; patterning black and white or bluish-white with rings around body and tail; head small; scales smooth; lips yellow; females larger than males

Habits Marine but comes ashore to bask, mate, and lay eggs; may climb cliffs and sleep under logs and rocks away from the shore

Breeding Egg layer with clutches of 6–18 eggs laid in sea caves; eggs hatch after 16–20 weeks

Diet Fish, almost entirely eels

Habitat Coral reefs and mangrove-covered coastlines

Distribution Southeast Asia and northern Australia

Status Numerous

Similar species Other *Laticauda* species, but this is the largest species; also the file snake, *Acrochordus granulatus*

Venom Very potent but rarely used on humans

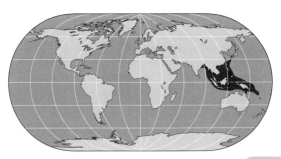

Sea Snakes

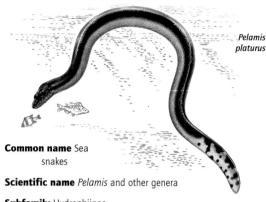

Pelamis platurus

Common name Sea snakes

Scientific name *Pelamis* and other genera

Subfamily Hydrophiinae

Family Elapidae

Suborder Serpentes

Order Squamata

Number of species 47–50 in 14 genera

Length From 18 in (45 cm) to 9 ft (2.7 m)

Key features Body flattened from side to side toward the tail, which is oar shaped; eyes small and usually placed on the side of the head; nostrils valvular and can be closed when diving; ventral scales greatly reduced; some species have small heads and thick bodies; various colors but often gray, brown, or olive; some have black-and-white bands; 1 species is bright yellow and black

Habits Exclusively marine

Breeding Live-bearers, giving birth at the water's surface

Diet Fish, crustaceans, and fish eggs

Habitat Open seas, estuaries, mud flats, mangrove forests, and tropical reefs

Distribution Northern Australia, the Indopacific region extending to the Arabian Gulf; *P. platurus* has a much wider distribution

Status Mostly common, sometimes numerous

Similar species Sea kraits have dark and light rings (as in some sea snakes) but less compressed bodies

Venom Depending on species, may be very potent; most species are reluctant to bite, but a few can be aggressive

all species
Pelamis platurus
occasional sightings of *Pelamis platurus*

Puff Adder

Common name
Puff adder

Scientific name
Bitis arietans

Subfamily Viperinae

Family Viperidae

Suborder Serpentes

Order Squamata

Length From 36 in (90 cm) to 6 ft (1.8 m)

Key features Body very stout with a large, broad head and rounded snout; scales heavily keeled; color varies slightly, but most have a dirty-yellow or brown body with large dark-gray, cream-edged chevrons or "u"-shaped markings down the back

Habits Terrestrial; nocturnal or diurnal depending on the weather and temperature

Breeding Live-bearer with large litters; the largest recorded was 156; gestation period about 90–120 days

Diet Mammals, birds, and lizards

Habitat Very adaptable; absent from closed canopy forest and from the most arid deserts, but otherwise it can occur anywhere

Distribution Africa south of the Sahara with an isolated population in southern Morocco; absent from the Congo Basin; a small population also occurs in the Arabian Peninsula

Status Very common

Similar species None; all other large adders have colorful geometric patterns

Venom Relatively toxic, but the main danger comes from the large amount injected, easily enough to kill a human; venom is slow acting, and with treatment over 90 percent of victims recover

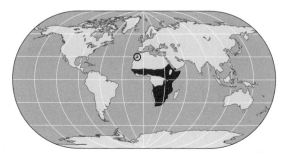

Gaboon Viper

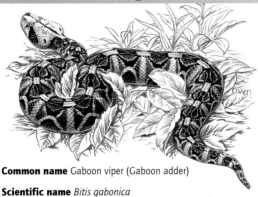

Common name Gaboon viper (Gaboon adder)

Scientific name *Bitis gabonica*

Subfamily Viperinae

Family Viperidae

Suborder Serpentes

Order Squamata

Length From 4 ft (1.2 m) to 6.6 ft (2 m)

Key features The longest and heaviest African viper with a massive girth and enormous, spade-shaped head; 1 pair of small hornlike scales on its snout, which are larger in individuals from West Africa (*B. g. rhinoceros*); its body is instantly recognizable with a pattern of geometrically arranged triangles, rectangles, and diamonds

Habits Terrestrial; active in the evening and at night

Breeding Live-bearer with litters of up to 60; gestation period about 90–120 days

Diet Small mammals

Habitat Tropical rain forest and open woodland

Distribution Central and West Africa with a few isolated populations in East and southeastern Africa

Status Common in suitable habitat

Similar species The rhinoceros viper, *B. nasicornis*, also has a pattern of brightly colored shapes

Venom Not particularly potent but injected in large quantities is easily enough to kill a human; bites very rare, however, because it is not often encountered and is apparently unlikely to bite even when stepped on

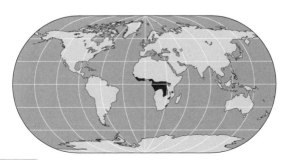

Sahara Horned Viper

Common name Sahara horned viper (desert horned viper)

Scientific name *Cerastes cerastes*

Subfamily Viperinae

Family Viperidae

Suborder Serpentes

Order Squamata

Length From 24 in (61 cm) to 34 in (86 cm)

Key features Body short and stocky; heavily keeled scales give it a roughened, matt appearance; there is a long spinelike scale (horn) over each eye, but hornless individuals also occur; the back is buff or sandy colored with ill-defined darker blotches along the center and smaller dark patches on each flank

Habits Terrestrial; nocturnal

Breeding Egg layer with clutches of 10–23 eggs that hatch after 42–56 days

Diet Lizards, small mammals, and birds

Habitat Desert; found across the Sahara on loose sand and sandy gravel

Distribution North Africa from the Sinai Desert to the Atlantic coast

Status Common

Similar species Two other species of *Cerastes*: *C. gasperettii* is found in the Arabian Peninsula; *C. vipera* lives in the Sahara but is smaller than *C. cerastes* and lacks horns

Venom Bites to humans are serious but rarely fatal

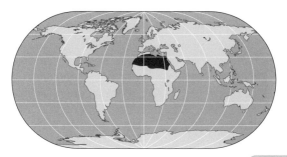

Carpet Vipers

Saw-scaled viper
(Echis carinatus)

Common name
Carpet vipers
(saw-scaled vipers)

Scientific name *Echis* sp.

Subfamily Viperinae

Family Viperidae

Suborder Serpentes

Order Squamata

Length From 20 in (50 cm) to 36 in (91 cm)

Key features Head rounded or pear shaped, covered with many small, keeled scales; eyes large and visible from above; pupils vertical; several rows of scales along the flanks have intricate patterns and serrated keels; color sandy brown, yellow, or gray to match the soil

Habits Mainly nocturnal; terrestrial, although occasionally climb into low bushes

Breeding Mostly egg layers, but at least 1 African population bears live young

Diet Varied from invertebrates to small mammals and birds

Habitat Semideserts, often where there are rocks; absent from the most arid sandy deserts

Distribution Large and disjointed from West and Central Africa through North Africa and the Middle East to Pakistan, India, and Sri Lanka

Status Common

Similar species All carpet vipers resemble each other, making identification difficult at times

Venom Potent, preventing blood from clotting and causing tissue damage; death can follow after several days without treatment

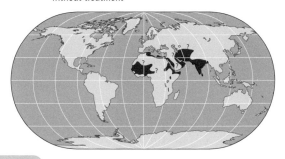

Nose-Horned Viper

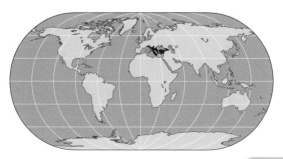

Common name Nose-horned viper
(sand viper and many
other local names)

Scientific name *Vipera ammodytes*

Subfamily Viperinae

Family Viperidae

Suborder Serpentes

Order Squamata

Length From 24 in (60 cm) to
35 in (90 cm)

Key features Distinctive nose horn
formed from 9–20 scales; body
color varies from silvery gray to
reddish brown but usually has a well-defined, dark-edged
zigzag down its back or a series of separate oval-shaped
markings; underside of the tail may be yellow, orange,
or red; males have more contrast in their markings
than females

Habits Usually diurnal but active in the early morning and
evening during very hot weather; terrestrial but quite
a good climber, sometimes exploring shrubs in search
of food

Breeding Live-bearer with litters of 4–20

Diet Mainly small mammals; also lizards and birds

Habitat Rocky places, especially hillsides

Distribution Europe from southern Austria (where it is rare)
across the Balkan region and into Turkey, Armenia,
Azerbaijan, and Georgia

Status Common in places

Similar species None within its range; several smaller European
vipers have upturned snouts, but none has a horn like
this species

Venom Highly toxic, causing swelling and pain; fatalities can
occur if bites go untreated

Adder

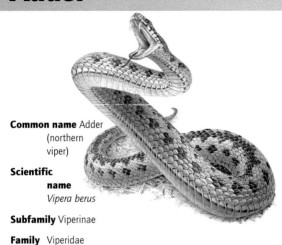

Common name Adder (northern viper)

Scientific name *Vipera berus*

Subfamily Viperinae

Family Viperidae

Suborder Serpentes

Order Squamata

Length From 24 in (61 cm) to 30 in (76 cm), exceptionally to 36 in (91 cm)

Key features Body stocky; head flat and covered with several large scales; dorsal scales are keeled, as in most vipers; basic pattern consists of a dark zigzag stripe on a lighter background, which may be gray, light brown, or reddish-brown; males' markings contrast more than those of females; melanistic (all-black) individuals are known; females are larger on average than males

Habits Diurnal; terrestrial, occasionally climbing into low bushes; swims well and may take to the water voluntarily

Breeding Live-bearer with litters of 3–18 young; gestation period about 112 days

Diet Small rodents, lizards, frogs, and invertebrates

Habitat Varied but typically dry meadows or dry sunny banks

Distribution Europe and Asia from the British Isles to the Pacific coast of Russia, north into Scandinavia, and south to northern France and Italy

Status Very common in places

Similar species Several other small vipers are similar

Venom Quite potent, but bites are very rarely fatal

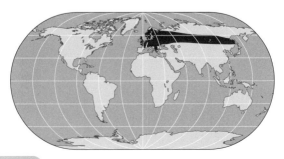

Copperhead

Common name Copperhead

Scientific name *Agkistrodon contortrix*

Subfamily Crotalinae

Family Viperidae

Suborder Serpentes

Order Squamata

Length From 24 in (61 cm) to 4 ft (1.2 m)

Key features Head triangular with large scales covering the top and a prominent facial pit; a number of broad, rich reddish-brown, chestnut, or coppery bars cross the body and become narrower toward the midline, like a bow tie, but the two sides often fail to meet perfectly, so they are staggered; background color is tan, and despite its name, the head is also tan color

Habits Terrestrial; nocturnal or diurnal according to season

Breeding Live-bearer with litters of 4–14; gestation period about 83–150 days

Diet Small mammals, lizards, amphibians, and invertebrates

Habitat Well-drained, lightly wooded places, including rocky hillsides and gardens, often near streams and ponds

Distribution Southeastern United States and adjacent parts of northeastern Mexico

Status Common

Similar species Some water snakes in the region are superficially similar, but their habitat is different, and they lack the facial pit

Venom Mildly dangerous; copperheads are placid and do not bite unless provoked

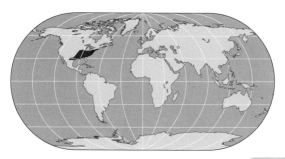

Eyelash Viper

Common name Eyelash viper (eyelash pit viper and other local names)

Scientific name *Bothriechis schlegelii*

Subfamily Crotalinae

Family Viperidae

Suborder Serpentes

Order Squamata

Length From 20 in (50 cm) to 30 in (76 cm)

Key features Cluster of raised scales above each eye; body fairly slender for a viper; tail prehensile; color highly variable but basically gray-green or golden yellow; color of pupil matches that of body

Habits Tree dwelling, although it sometimes descends to the ground

Breeding Live-bearer with litters of 6–24 small young; gestation period about 140–168 days

Diet Frogs, lizards, birds, and small mammals

Habitat Rain forests; in Central America it is a lowland and foothill species living to about 4,500 ft (1,400 m), but in South America it is found at higher elevations up to 8,000 ft (2,400 m)

Distribution Central America and northern South America

Status Common in suitable habitats

Similar species Other tree pit vipers in the region, but none have the raised scales above the eyes

Venom Bites quite common, and a small proportion are fatal

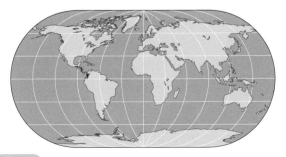

Terciopelo

Common name Terciopelo (fer-de-lance, lancehead, tommygoff, and many other local names)

Scientific name *Bothrops asper*

Subfamily Crotalinae

Family Viperidae

Suborder Serpentes

Order Squamata

Length From 4 ft (1.2 m) to 8 ft (2.5 m)

Key features Body large and stocky; head triangular; snout pointed; color variable but usually tan or brown with pale-bordered triangles down each flank meeting across the back or alternating with each other

Habits Nocturnal; terrestrial, although juveniles may be partially arboreal

Breeding Live-bearer with large litters

Diet Mammals, birds, lizards, mice, and invertebrates

Habitat Rain forests, clearings, banana plantations, and fields

Distribution Central and northern South America from the Atlantic coast of Mexico through the Yucatán Peninsula and Central America and into western Venezuela and northern Ecuador

Status Very common (and probably becoming more common)

Similar species Other terrestrial pit vipers, notably the common lancehead, *B. atrox*

Venom A potent and deadly hemotoxin

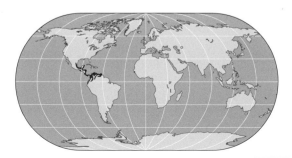

Bushmasters

Lachesis muta

Common name Bushmasters (matabueys)

Scientific name *Lachesis* sp.

Subfamily Crotalinae

Family Viperidae

Suborder Serpentes

Order Squamata

Number of species 3

Length Up to 10 ft (3 m), exceptionally to over 11 ft (3. 3 m)

Key features Massive vipers; body with heavily keeled scales giving a knobby appearance; backbone forms a prominent ridge; head large and rounded; distinct facial pits between nostrils and eyes; color usually yellow, tan, or pinkish with sooty black, roughly diamond-shaped marking down the back; some variation in marking across the 3 species

Habits Terrestrial; nocturnal

Breeding Egg layers, with clutches of 5–18 eggs; eggs hatch after about 60 days

Diet Mammals, especially spiny rats when available

Habitat Rain forests

Distribution Central and South America, with gaps between populations

Status Common to rare; population on the southeastern Brazilian coast, *L. muta rhombeata*, is endangered

Similar species The 3 species are similar to each other but unlike any other snakes

Venom Extremely toxic; 75 percent of bite victims die even with medical attention

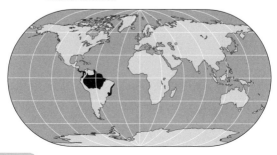

Western Diamond-Back Rattlesnake

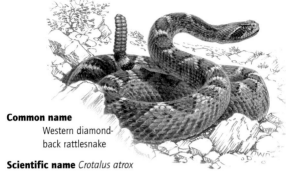

Common name
Western diamond-back rattlesnake

Scientific name *Crotalus atrox*

Subfamily Crotalinae

Family Viperidae

Suborder Serpentes

Order Squamata

Length From 30 in (76 cm) to 7 ft (2.1 m)

Key features Body has large diamond-shaped markings along the back, each outlined with lighter scales; background color gray to brown, may be reddish brown or pink; head large and rounded with a wide dark stripe from the eye to the angle of the jaws; tail conspicuously banded in black and white, ending in a large rattle (series of horny segments made of keratin)

Habits Nocturnal in summer but active in late afternoon and early morning in the spring and fall; terrestrial

Breeding Live-bearer with litters of 4–25

Diet Small mammals up to the size of young prairie dogs and rabbits

Habitat Desert, semidesert, arid scrub, and dry grassland

Distribution North America almost from coast to coast; ranges from southeastern California and the Gulf of California to the Gulf Coast of Texas and south into Mexico

Status Very common in places

Similar species The Mojave rattlesnake, *C. scutulatus*, is very similar, and its range overlaps in places

Venom A potent hemotoxin leading to severe symptoms and possibly death unless treated

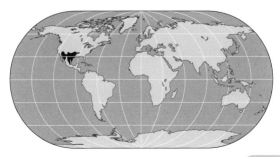

Sidewinder

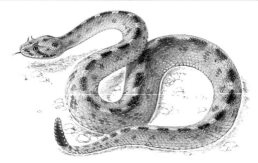

Common name Sidewinder (horned rattlesnake)

Scientific name *Crotalus cerastes*

Subfamily Crotalinae

Family Viperidae

Suborder Serpentes

Order Squamata

Length From 24 in (61 cm) to 30 in (76 cm)

Key features Body smaller and more slender than other rattlesnakes; head flat with raised scales over the eyes, giving the appearance of horns; pattern consists of large blotches of various colors interspersed with dark speckles; background coloration varies with the soil type and may be yellow, beige, pink, or gray

Habits Terrestrial; semiburrowing by shuffling its body down into loose sand; active at night; moves in a sideways looping motion

Breeding Live-bearer with litters of 5–18; gestation period 150 days or more

Diet Mainly lizards, especially whiptails; also small rodents

Habitat Deserts, especially where there are extensive dunes of loose, wind-blown sand

Distribution Southwestern North America

Status Common

Similar species The speckled rattlesnake, *C. mitchelli*, has a larger rattle, but it lives mostly among rocks and does not sidewind

Venom Not very potent, causing pain and swelling around the site of the wound

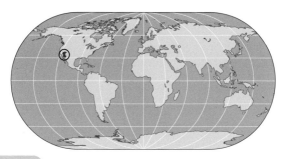

Massasauga

Common name Massasauga

Scientific name *Sistrurus catenatus*

Subfamily Crotalinae

Family Viperidae

Suborder Serpentes

Order Squamata

Length From 30 in (76 cm) to 36 in (91 cm)

Key features Small with a tiny rattle; head has large plates on top, distinguishing all *Sistrurus* species from *Crotalus*; body has row of large round dark-brown blotches down its back; flanks have smaller spots; background color grayish or brown; some individuals from northern parts may be suffused with black

Habits Terrestrial; diurnal in cool places, becoming more nocturnal in the south

Breeding Live-bearer with litters of 2–19; gestation period 71–115 days

Diet Small lizards, mice, and invertebrates

Habitat Desert grassland, bogs, and forest edges

Distribution Central North America from southeastern Arizona and northern Mexico to New York State

Status Rare

Similar species Once the rattle has been seen or heard, it cannot be mistaken for any other snake; some snakes, such as the western hognose, *Heterodon nasicus*, are similar in size, color, and markings

Venom Very toxic, but yields are small; symptoms include local swelling, intense pain, and nausea

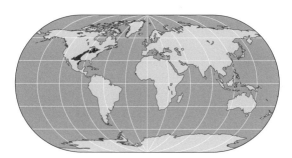

Tuataras

Sphenodon punctatus

Common name Tuataras

Scientific name *Sphenodon punctatus* and *S. guntheri*

Family Sphenodontidae

Order Rhynchocephalia

Size From 20 in (50 cm) to 31 in (80 cm) long; males larger than females

Key features Body squat; color of adults olive-green, gray, or black with a speckling of gray, yellow, or white; newly hatched animals are brown or gray with pink tinges; head has a pink shield and striped throat; sometimes distinctive light patches occur on the body and tail

Habits Nocturnal burrowers

Breeding Egg layers; average clutch size from 6 to 10; incubation period about 11–15 months

Diet Invertebrates such as beetles, crickets, and spiders; also the eggs and chicks of seabirds; frogs, lizards, and young tuataras also eaten occasionally

Habitat Low forest and scrub usually associated with colonies of burrowing seabirds

Distribution About 33 small islands and rock stacks off the coast of New Zealand

Status *S. guntheri* is listed as Vulnerable (IUCN); *S. punctatus* has a very limited range

Similar species None

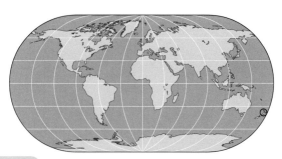

Gharial

Common name Gharial

Scientific name *Gavialis gangeticus*

Subfamily Gavialinae

Family Crocodylidae

Order Crocodylia

Size Up to 21 feet (6.4 m) long overall

Weight Large males may weigh up to 1 ton (1,016 kg)

Key features Body relatively slim with an elongated, narrow snout; in males snout has a knob at its tip; teeth narrow, sharp, and interlocking; color usually olive-green with dark bands across the body; rear feet heavily webbed

Habits Highly aquatic

Breeding Female lays clutch of 28–43 eggs; eggs hatch after 65 or 80 days

Diet Predominantly fish; older individuals may also catch birds; reputedly scavenges on the cremated remains of humans

Habitat Rivers

Distribution Northern parts of the Indian subcontinent

Status Endangered (IUCN); listed on CITES Appendix I

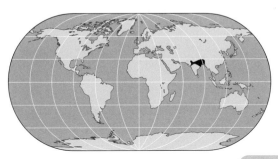

American Alligator

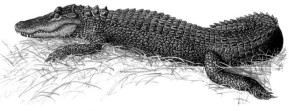

Common name American alligator

Scientific name *Alligator mississippiensis*

Subfamily Alligatorinae

Family Crocodylidae

Order Crocodylia

Size Large specimens measure up to 13 ft (4 m) long; reports of individuals up to 20 ft (6 m) long are unsubstantiated

Weight Can exceed 550 lb (249 kg)

Key features Body almost black; snout relatively long, wide, and rounded; front feet have 5 toes on each; hind feet have 4; when the mouth is closed, only upper teeth visible (which distinguishes alligators from crocodiles)

Habits Active during the summer; may hibernate during the winter, especially in northern areas; semiaquatic, emerging to bask on land; can move quite fast on land and will search for new habitat when pools dry up

Breeding Female lays clutches of 30–70 eggs; hatchlings emerge after about 2 months

Diet Carnivorous; feeds on prey ranging from crustaceans to much larger aquatic life, including fish, turtles, and wading birds, as well as mammals

Habitat Rivers, marshland, and swamps; sometimes in brackish water; rarely seen at sea

Distribution Southeastern United States from Texas to Florida and north through the Carolinas

Status Delisted from being an endangered species in 1985, having been the subject of a successful recovery program; listed on CITES Appendix II

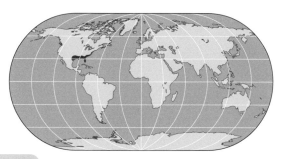

Black Caiman

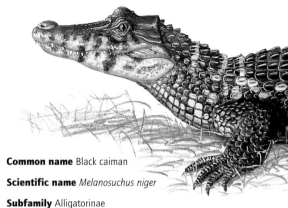

Common name Black caiman

Scientific name *Melanosuchus niger*

Subfamily Alligatorinae

Family Crocodylidae

Order Crocodylia

Size Up 20 ft (6.1 m), making it the largest of all South American crocodilians

Weight Approximately 500 lb (227 kg)

Key features Body black with dots that are especially evident in young hatchlings; head gray in youngsters, becoming reddish-brown as they age; snout relatively wide at the base, rapidly narrowing along its length; an obvious bony ridge is evident above the eyes, continuing down the snout; protective body casing on the neck and back is the thickest of all crocodilians

Habits Nocturnal hunter; often encountered in flooded areas of forest during the wet season

Breeding Female produces clutch of 50–60 eggs that are deposited in a nest mound; eggs hatch after 6 weeks

Diet Young feed on aquatic invertebrates and small fish; larger individuals eat bigger prey, including some mammals

Habitat Shallow areas of water in rain-forest areas

Distribution Confined to the Amazon drainage basin; appears to be conspicuously absent from Surinam

Status Has declined in many parts of its range as the result of heavy hunting for the leather trade during the second half of the 20th century; IUCN Lower Risk; CITES Appendices I and II

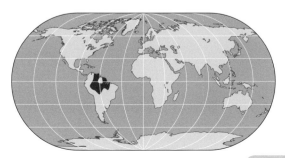

Saltwater Crocodile

Common name Saltwater crocodile (Indopacific crocodile, estuarine crocodile)

Scientific name *Crocodylus porosus*

Subfamily Crocodylinae

Family Crocodylidae

Order Crocodylia

Size At least 23 feet (7 m) long; possibly up to 30 feet (9 m), but this is unconfirmed

Weight Possibly in excess of 2,418 lb (1,097 kg)

Key features Broad, powerful snout and strong jaws; a ridge runs from each eye toward the center of the snout; usually quite light in color when adult with overall gray or tan coloration; darker banding may be apparent on the tail with the smooth underparts creamy yellow; young are more colorful with clearer contrast between light and dark areas; has less bony protection on the head shield than any other living species of crocodile

Habits Highly aggressive predator; powerful swimmer; diurnal

Breeding Female lays 1 clutch of 60–80 eggs and guards them until they hatch after about 3 months

Diet Hatchlings prey on small aquatic animals; adults eat larger prey ranging from buffalo to sharks

Habitat Found in a variety of environments from rivers, lakes, and swamps to the open ocean

Distribution Eastern India, Southeast Asia, Papua New Guinea, Australia, and other Pacific islands

Status Relatively common; numbers have increased in some areas thanks to protective measures; IUCN Lower Risk; CITES Appendices I and II

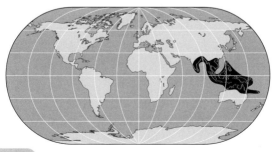

Nile Crocodile

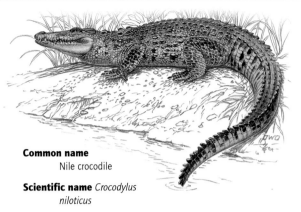

Common name
Nile crocodile

Scientific name *Crocodylus niloticus*

Subfamily Crocodylinae

Family Crocodylidae

Order Crocodylia

Size Largest official record is 19.5 ft (6 m) from snout to tail; large specimens today are usually no longer than 16 ft (4.9 m)

Weight Up to 2,300 lb (1,043 kg)

Key features Appearance variable, leading to the identification of numerous subspecies; body usually dark, sometimes blackish, with lighter underparts; young are olive-brown with blackish markings across the body; mouthparts broad and powerful

Habits Large individuals are aggressive and dangerous, seizing prey at the water's edge; uses speed and stealth for hunting; diurnal; sometimes basks on shore

Breeding Female usually lays 16–80 eggs in a clutch depending on age and subspecies; nest guarding known in both sexes; eggs hatch after about 2 months

Diet Young hatchlings feed largely on aquatic creatures, including invertebrates and amphibians; adults take much larger prey, including giraffes and even humans

Habitat Usually restricted to freshwater habitats; may be found on beaches and occasionally at sea

Distribution Africa, occurring over a very wide area south and east of the Sahara; also found on the island of Zanzibar

Status Some decline in local populations but relatively common overall; listed on CITES Appendices I and II

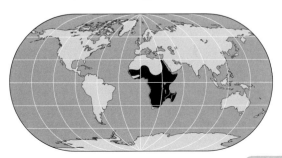

Glossary

Words in SMALL CAPITALS refer to other entries in the glossary.

Amplexus position adopted during mating in most frogs and many salamanders, in which the male clasps the female with one or both pairs of limbs. See AXILLARY AMPLEXUS and INGUINAL AMPLEXUS

Arboreal living in the branches of trees or shrubs

Axillary amplexus mating position in which the male grasps the female behind her front limbs. See INGUINAL AMPLEXUS

Barbel a small, elongated "feeler," or sensory process, on the head, usually aquatic animals, e.g., some pipid frogs

Calcareous containing calcium carbonate

Carapace the upper part of the shell of turtles and tortoises. Also used to describe the hard structure covering part of any animal's body

CITES Convention on International Trade in Endangered Species. Restricts international trade by licensing controls. Rare animals and plants listed in Appendices: I—endangered and most restricted trade; II—not endangered but could be if trade not restricted; III—least restricted trade

Class taxonomic category ranking below phylum and above ORDER

Cloaca the chamber into which the urinary, digestive, and reproductive systems discharge their contents, and which opens to the exterior

Clutch the eggs laid by a female at one time

Costal grooves grooves or folds along the flanks of caecilians and some salamanders that correspond to the position of the ribs

Crepuscular active at dusk

Cryptic having the ability to remain hidden, usually by means of camouflage, e.g., cryptic coloration

Dewlap flap or fold of skin under an animal's throat. Sometimes used in displays

Direct development transition from egg to the adult form in amphibians without passing through a free-living larval stage

Dorsal relating to the back or upper surface of the body or one of its parts

Eft juvenile, TERRESTRIAL phase in the life cycle of a newt. The red eft is the terrestrial juvenile form of the eastern newt, *Notophthalmus viridescens*

Elliptical (pupils) shaped like an ellipse, as in the pupils of some snakes and lizards

Endemic restricted to a particular geographical region

Estivation state of inactivity during prolonged periods of high temperature or drought—an animal may bury itself in soil or mud

Estuarine living in the lower part of a river (estuary) where fresh water meets and mixes with seawater

Explosive breeder a species in which the breeding season is very short, resulting in large numbers of animals mating at the same time

External fertilization fusing of eggs and sperm outside the female's body, as in nearly all frogs and toads. See INTERNAL FERTILIZATION

Family taxonomic category ranking below ORDER, containing GENERA that are more closely related to one another than any other grouping of genera

Genus (pl. genera) taxonomic category ranking below FAMILY; a group of SPECIES more closely related to each other than to any other group of species

Gestation carrying the developing young within the body. Gestation period is the length of time that this occurs

Gill respiratory structure in aquatic animals through which gas exchange takes place

Granular (scale) small grainlike scales covering the body, as in some geckos

Gular pouch area of expandable skin in the throat region

Heat pits pits containing cells sensitive to heat, located between the eye and nose or along the edges of the jaws in some snakes; used to detect prey

Herbivore animal that eats plants

Hibernation a period of inactivity, often spent underground, to avoid extremes of cold

Hinge a means by which the PLASTRON of some chelonians can be pulled up, giving the reptile more protection against a would-be predator

Hood an expansion of the area around the head in some reptiles to make themselves appear larger; in cobras it is created by flattening the ribs of the neck

Inguinal amplexus mating position in which a male frog or salamander clasps a female around the lower abdomen. See AXILLARY AMPLEXUS

Intergular scute a single plate, or SCUTE, lying between the paired gular scutes on the PLASTRON of side-necked turtles

Internal fertilization fusing of eggs and sperm inside the female's body, as in reptiles and most salamanders. See EXTERNAL FERTILIZATION

Introduced species brought from lands where it occurs naturally to lands where it has not previously occurred

IUCN International Union for the Conservation of Nature, responsible for assigning animals and plants to internationally agreed categories of rarity. *See* table below

Juvenile young animal, not sexually mature

Karst a porous form of limestone

Keeled scales a ridge on the DORSAL scales of some snakes

Lifestyle general mode of life of an animal, e.g., NOCTURNAL predator, aquatic HERBIVORE, parasite

Live-bearing giving birth to young that have developed beyond the egg stage

Lure (noun) part of the body, such as the tail, that is used to entice prey closer

Metamorphosis transformation of an animal from one stage of its life history to another, e.g., from LARVA to adult

Montane pertaining to mountains or SPECIES that live in mountains

Neoteny condition in which a LARVA fails to METAMORPHOSE and retains its larval features as an adult. Species with this condition are said to be neotenic. The axolotl is the best-known example

Newt amphibious salamanders of the genera *Triturus*, *Taricha*, and *Notophthalmus*

Nocturnal active at night

Ocellus (pl. ocelli) a simple eye with a single lens

Omnivore an animal that eats both animal and plant material

Order taxonomic category ranking below CLASS and above FAMILY

Osteoderm small bone in the skin of some reptiles; lies under the scales

Overwinter survive the winter

Parotid glands pair of large glands on the shoulder, neck, or behind the eye in some salamanders and toads

Plastron the ventral portion, or underside, of the shell of a turtle

Prehensile adapted for grasping or clasping, especially by wrapping around, such as the tail of chameleons

Saxicolous living or growing among rocks

Savanna open grassland with scattered trees and bushes

Scute enlarged scale on a reptile, including the colorful scales that cover the shell of turtles; divided into different groups, such as the vertebral scutes that run above the vertebral column

Species taxonomic category ranking below GENUS; a group of organisms with common attributes capable of interbreeding and producing healthy fertile offspring

Sphagnum type of moss that grows only in wet, acid areas; their remains become compacted peat other plant debris to form peat

Subspecies a locally distinct group of animals that differ slightly from the normal appearance of the SPECIES; often called a race

Tadpole LARVAL stage of a frog or toad

Terrestrial living on land

Thermoregulation control of body temperature by behavioral or physiological means, so that it maintains a constant or near-constant value

Tubercle small, knoblike projection

Tympanum (pl. tympana) eardrum

Vent the CLOACAL opening of the body. Measurements of reptiles and amphibians are often given as "snout-vent" lengths or "s-v" lengths

Ventral relating to the lower surface of the body or one of its parts

Vertical (pupils) the shape of the pupils in some snakes and lizards, enabling them to lie beneath the surface with the top part of the head exposed, while retaining the ability to see above the surface

Vestigial smaller and of more simple structure than in an evolutionary ancestor. In reptiles and amphibians often used to describe limbs that have become reduced in size through the evolutionary process

Vocal sac in some male frogs an area around the throat that fills with air in order to amplify the sound when calling for a mate

IUCN CATEGORIES

EX **Extinct,** when there is no reasonable doubt that the last individual of the species has died.	**LR** **Lower Risk** (before 2001)/**NT** **Near Threatened** (since 2001), when a species has been evaluated and does not satisfy the criteria for CR, EN, or VU.
EW **Extinct in the Wild,** when a species is known only to survive in captivity or as a naturalized population well outside the past range.	**LC** **Least Concern** (since 2001), when an animal has been evaluated and does not qualify for CR, EN, VU, LR, or NT.
CR **Critically Endangered,** when a species is facing an extremely high risk of extinction in the wild in the immediate future.	**DD** **Data Deficient,** when there is not enough information about a species to assess the risk of extinction.
EN **Endangered,** when a species is facing a very high risk of extinction in the wild in the near future.	**NE** **Not Evaluated,** species that have not been assessed by the IUCN criteria.
VU **Vulnerable,** when a species is facing a high risk of extinction in the wild in the medium-term future.	

Index